HENRY COUNTY, VIRGINIA

In October, 1776 the General Assembly of Virginia passed an act to divide the County of Pittsylvania into two distinct Counties; based on the representation to the Assembly by sundry inhabitants of the County of Pittsylvania that from the great extent of the County and their remote situation from the Courthouse, they were subject to great inconvenience.

The act referred to above specified that after the last day of December of the year 1776, Pittsylvania should be divided into two counties and that the new county should be named "Henry County" for the celebrated Patrick Henry, the first Governor of Virginia who later lived in this county.

Henry County, when first formed, embraced not only its present limits, but the whole of what is now Patrick County and the greater portion of the present county of Franklin as well.

The act of the General Assembly of Virginia forming the county was followed by another act to establish the places and time of holding courts in the counties of Pittsylvania and Henry. This act specified that for Pittsylvania at the House of Richard Farthing on the fourth Thursday in January and for the County of Henry at the house of John Rowland on the third Monday in January.

Those appointed by Governor Patrick Henry to be Justices of Henry County's first court included among others Col. Abraham Penn and Col. George Waller both of whom had served in the Revolutionary War and were with General Washington at the surrender of Lord Cornwallis at Yorktown.

Edwin P. Waller,
Martinsville, Virginia.

CONTENTS

		Page
1.	Marriage Bonds Listed with Husbands' Names Alphabetized	1
2.	Wives' Names Alphabetized for Cross Reference	61
3.	Ministers' Returns with Husbands' Names Alphabetized	84

May 9, 1818	Abington, Wm. F., and Fanny Shelton.
May 12, 1849	Abington, William M., and Mary J. Philpott, dau. of David Philpott.
Feb. 8, 1801	Adams, Randolph, and Saley Herndon.
Apr. 5, 1813	Adams, William P., and Nancy Ramey, dau. of Sanford Reamey, Sr.
Oct. 16, 1827	Adkisson, John W., and Martha Ann Staples, dau. of Ruth H. Staples.
Apr. 28, 1800	Agee, Jacob, and Ailsey Burchett, by consent of Keziah Burchett.
May 17, 1814	Agee, Lewis, and Patey Wells, dau. of Thomas Wells.
Dec. 12, 1823	Agee, Pleasant, and Nancy Rogers.
Sept. 9, 1803	Agee, William, and Elizabeth Pursell, dau. of John Pursell.
Nov. 23, 1840	Aistrop, John, and Sarah Gilbert.
Sept. 21, 1842	Aistrop, Oliver P., son of John Aistrop, and Sally Faris, dau. of Daniel Faris.
Jan. 20, 1834	Aistrop, Robert G., and Elizabeth Moore, dau. of Alexander and Elizabeth Moore.
May 17, 1800	Akin, Michael, and Mary Davis, dau. of John Davis.
May 30, 1803	Aken, Thomas, and Polley Chapman, dau. of Thomas Chapman.
Jan. 14, 1800	Alexander, Ingram, and Elizabeth Nunn.
Mar. 4, 1807	Alexander, Joseph, and Nancy Bouldin, by consent of Jos. Bouldin.
Dec. 24, 1798	Alexander, Martin, and Winney Jones, by consent of Henry Jones.
Jan. 24, 1804	Alexander, Robert, and Mary Miller.
Feb. 21, 1778	Alexander, William, and Jean Farguson.
Sept. 12, 1831	Alison, Robert, and Mary L. Christian.
Dec. 5, 1827	Allen, Coleman, and Frances Deshazo, dau. of William Deshazo.
Dec. 23, 1835	Allen, David M., and Sally Ann Spencer, dau. of Wm. Spencer.

Jan. 9, 1837   Allen, Jones, and Susan F. Minter, dau. of Obadiah Minter.

Sept. 30, 1807   Allen, Joseph, and Sally Wade.

Sept, 5, 1807   Allen, Pines, and Charlotte Bailey, by consent of Parks Bailey.

July 9, 1821   Allen, Pines, and Nancy W. Hughes.

Oct. 24, 1803   Allen, Robert, and Ceally Mullins, dau. of David Mullins.

Dec. 4, 1811   Allen, William, and Patsy Jones.

Apr. 19, 1800   Ammerman, Stephen, and ------- ------

May 13, 1797   Anderson, John, and Elizabeth Walker, dau. of Thomas Walker

Nov. 4, 1841   Anderson, Leonard W. ("under 21 years of age"), and Martha A. Fontaine. Hugh F. Morton, of Pr. Ed. Co., grdn. of husband.

Sept. 4, 1794   Anderson, Robert, and Elizabeth Graves, dau. of Mary Graves.

Dec. 14, 1818   Anderson, Robert, and Nancy Jones.

May 25, 1845   Anderson, Seward G., and Nancy Hopper, dau. of James Hopper

Apr. 12, 1841   Anglin, Philip, and Parthenia E. Mills, dau. of James B. Mills

Feb. 12, 1800   Anglin, Samuel, and Caty Coursey.

Mar. 24, 1842   Archer, Joseph, and Rachel Feazle, dau. of Aaron Feazel.

May 8, 1810   Armistead, Francis, and Sally Hale, dau. of William Hale.

Jan. 26, 1807   Armistead, Samuel, and Sally Martin, dau. of Jos. Martin.

Oct. 22, 1821   Arnn, Henry (of Pittsylvania Co.), and Nancy Martin, dau. of Orson Martin.

Dec. 16, 1813   Arnold, Lewis, and Hannah Philpott.

Feb. 21, 1825   Arnold, James, and Julia Barrow.

Feb. 8, 1813   Arthur, David, and Gincy Grigg.

May 22, 1834   Artis, Jeff ("free man of color"), and Ann Cousins ("free woman of color").

Oct. 1, 1835   Ashby, Shelton, and ----- -----

May 7, 1816   Athey, Benjamin, and Jean Cheatham.

July 29, 1837   Athy, James, and Mary Ann Hay, dau. of Peter Hay.

Sept. 13, 1841   Atkins, John, and Lucinda D. Stultz.

Dec. 24, 1807   Atkinson, Jessee, and Polley Williams, dau. of
Garrott Williams.

Dec. 12, 1826   Austin, Daniel B., and Mary A. Hankins, by consent of
Wm. Hankins.

Jan. 31, 1822   Austin, Garland A., and Eliza. J. Hankins, by consent
of William Hankins.

July 13, 1835   Austin, Jefferson, and Ann S. Hankins, by consent of
William Hankins.

Jan. 7, 1825   Austin, John, and Oney Allen, by consent of
Meredith Allen.

Oct. 12, 1829   Ayers, Murphey, and Eliza Wells, dau. of Reuben Wells.

Mar. 18, 1792   Bailey, John, and Lydia Wilson.

Dec. 25, 1831   Baker, George, and Elizabeth Dillion, dau. of
William Dillion.

Feb. - 1813   Baker, Jeremiah, and Milly Pace, dau. of Jno. Pace.

Apr. 3, 1802   Baker, Thomas, and Jamima Baker.

Aug. 7, 1795   Baley, James Baul, and Nancy Roach, dau. of
Winiford Roach, consent only.

Feb. 12, 1830   Barber, Carter, and Winfred Jones, dau. of A. Jones.

May 11, 1840   Barber, Carter, and Mariah Estis.

Oct. 10, 1827   Barber, Seth, and Pitsey B. Jones.

May 7, 1838   Barding, John M., and Jane E. Martin, dau. of
Orson Martin.

Mar. 15, 1802   Barger, Peter, and Hamar (?) Hefflefinger.

Mar. 7, 1836   Barker, Burwell, son of Joseph Barker, and Jane McDaniel.

May 2, 1838   Barker, Gwilliams, and Sarah Barker. Allen Barker,
consent for husband and wife.

Nov. 15, 1836   Barker, Joseph, and Virginia Lemmons, dau. of
Jefferson Lemons.

Dec. 7, 1803   Barksdale, Wm., and Salley Smith.

Dec. 19, 1832   Barnett, Thomas, and Martha Casey, dau. of Martha Casey.

Mar. 6, 1843   Barrow, David, and Chancy Davis, dau. of George Davis.

Mar. 9, 1818   Barrow, Jessee, and Elizabeth Thomason.

Oct. 15, 1839   Barrow, William M., and Elizabeth J. King, dau. of
Christiana King.

Jan. 24, 1793   Bassett, Burrell, and Polly Hunter, dau. of Alex. Hunter.

Aug. 21, 1818   Bassett, Burwell W., and Martha Bassett.

Oct. 18, 1841   Bassett, Burwell, and Malinda Waller.

May 26, 1829   Bassett, William N., and Jane O. Staples.

Dec. 26, 1843   Bateman, John, and Eliza Jane Cahall, dau. of
Barney Cahall.

Aug. 19, 1819   Bateman, Azel, and Levina Gilley, dau. of George Gilley.

Aug. 15, 1846   Bateman, George, and Mary Rebecca Grant, dau. of
Archibald Grant.

Apr. 12, 1793   Bayles, William, and ----- -----

Nov. 26, 1804   Bays, Isaiah, and Jeany Hunter, by consent of Titus Hunter.

Jan. 12, 1801   Bays, Jesse, and Betsey Hunter, by consent of Titus Hunter.

Dec. 15, 1842   Beale, William, Jr., and Mary Rowland, grdn.
Mathew Seay.

Jan. 26, 1798   Beck, John, and Ann Scales.

Dec. 14, 1807   Beck, Levy, and Bettsey McCullock.

Apr. 24, 1809   Beheler, John, and Milley Mullins, dau. of Richard Mullins.

Dec. 28, 1833   Bell, George W., and Winney Watson, dau. of
Stinson (?) Watson.

Mar. 8, 1841   Bell, Nathan, and Milley Minter.

Dec. 25, 1794   Belleman, William, and Nelly Molin.

Apr. 6, 1782   Bernard, Walter, and Ruth Hill.

Jan. 23, 1827   Bird, Abner, and Sarah Brewer, consent of Nancy Brewer.

Dec. 17, 1826   Bird, Marshall, and Mary J. Allen, dau. of Pines Allen.

Sept. 13, 1819   Bird, James, and Eurelia (?) Philpott.

Oct. 9, 1837   Bird, Lewis, and Frances Draper.

Apr. 2, 1829   Bishop, James, and Zaporah Taylor, dau. of John Taylor.

Feb. 15, 1841   Bishop, William, and Sarah Carter, dau. of Philip Carter.

Aug. 2, 1780   Blakey, Churchill, and Agnes Anthony, dau. of Joseph Anthony.

July 12, 1780   Bledsoe, Peachy, and Pegy George.

Dec. 28, 1845   Boaz, Stephen M., and Sarah E. Taylor.

Jan. 5, 1830   Bocock, Drury, and Sally Dorson.

Dec. 12, 1831   Booker, Edward, and Martha Ann Sheffield, dau. of Leond. Sheffield.

Aug. 15, 1842   Booth, George, and Mary J. Pruette.

Feb. 22, 1842   Booth, Moses G., and Anna E. S. Redd.

Oct. 1, 1832   Bondurant, James, and Margaret Bocock.

Jan. 20, 1834   Bouldin, Frederick H., and Mildred P, Rea, consent of David Rea.

May 25, 1807   Bouldin, Joseph, Jr., and Patsey Royster, consent of Elizabeth Royster.

Dec. 11, 1837   Bouldin, Obediah C., and Ann R. Wells.

Nov. 29, 1817   Bouldin, Richard T., and Sally East, dau. of Thos. East.

Jan. 25, 1808   Bouldin, Thomas C., and Anna Hardin Scales.

Mar. 19, 1809   Bouldin, William, and Nancy B. Weaver.

May 30, 1821   Bowles, Alexander H., and Catherine Goode.

Apr. 27, 1795   Bowles, John, and Fanny Bolling.

Dec. 17, 1842	Bowles, John, and Mary Edwards, dau. of Mary Edwards.
May 9, 1846	Bowles, Joseph, and Lucinda Robertson.
Jan. 8, 1839	Bowles, Lewis, and Frances Nunn.
Apr. 15, 1841	Bradberry, Peter, and Elizabeth B. Feazle, dau. of Aaron Feazle.
Sept. 8, 1835	Bradberry, Richard, and Judith Dillon.
Mar. 20, 1814	Bradbury, James, and Elizabeth Dent, dau. of Shadric Dent.
Jan. 2, 1818	Bradbury, Mark, and Nancy Hardy.
Nov. 21, 1819	Bray, John, and Sarah Johnston.
Nov. 19, 1838	Bray, John, and Lucy Hankins.
Oct. 14, 1839	Brewer, John S., and Maria Ann Bottom.
Oct. 1, 1796	Brewer, William, and Nancy Morriss, dau. of Sam Morriss.
Oct. 4, 1836	Brewer, William P., and Martha S. Waller, consent of George Waller.
Mar. 15, 1845	Briant, James, and Martha Harger.
Jan. 24, 1799	Bridel, Enock, and Mary Cothrin.
Dec. 28, 1829	Brim, David, and Michy Pratt, dau. of John and Nancy Pratt.
Dec. 13, 1824	Brim, Nicholas, and Elizabeth Hill, dau. of Maning Hill.
Dec. 22, 1782	Briscoe, Truman, and Chaterine Dunn, dau. of Waters Dunn.
Sept. 28, 1801	Brown, Starling, and Susanna Clark.
Sept. 17, 1849	Brown, Thomas, and Lucy Beck, dau. of Levi Beck.
Feb. 1, 1849	Brown, William, and Ann A. Stuart, dau. of David Stuart.
Feb. 16, 1825	Bryant, Banister, son of Eley Bryant, and Biddy Wray, dau. of Lovesay Wray.
July 30, 1798	Bryant, Eli, and Mary Weatherford.
Oct. 2, 1839	Bryant, Elisha, and Lucy Hundley.

Apr. 19, 1816   Bundurant, John, and Lucy Gilley.

Dec. 11, 1799   Burch, Basil, and Mary Edwards, consent of
Joshua Proctor.

Oct. 10, 1829   Burch, Bazel, and Martha -·----

Dec. 4, 1836   Burch, Gerrard, and Elinor Richardson, dau of
John Richardson.

Dec. 19, 1838   Burch, James, and Sintha Minter, dau. of Silas Minter.

Oct. 9, 1844   Burch, James, and Nancy Richardson, dau. of
John Richardson.

Dec. 1, 1827   Burch, John, and Lucy Perkinson.

June 8, 1813   Burchett, Bartlett, and Nancy Mauldin.

June 3, 1807   Burchett, Benjamin, and Caty Vaughan.

Oct. 18, 1812   Burchett, Lenord, and Nancy Meredith.

Nov. 9, 1818   Burchett, Thos., and Susannah Meredith.

Jan. 26, 1794   Burgess, David, and Lucy Pace, dau. of John Pace.

Nov. 10, 1823   Burgess, Davis, and -·---- Lanier.

Jan. 25, 1808   Burgess, Harrison, and Jeanny Akin.

Oct. 22, 1825   Burgess, John, and Polley Weaver.

Feb. 9, 1837   Burgess, John, and Matilda France, dau. of
Nancy France.

Nov. 31, 1849   Burgess, John W., and Martha J. Jones.

Oct. 15, 1804   Burgess, Pendleton, and Rebeccah Griggs, dau. of
John Griggs, Sr.

Nov. 30, 1795   Burnett, John, and Lucy Allen Brock, granddau. of
George Brock "with whom she linves."

Jan. 12, 1795   Burnett, William, and Dosha Quarles, consent of
Francis Quarles.

Jan. 3, 1803   Burris, Jacob, and Ruth Dillion, dau. of Phebe Dillen.

Mar. 13, 1781   Burruss, Jacob, and Susanah Martin, dau. of
Joseph Martin.

Mar. 14, 1814   Burton, Robert P., and Lucy B. Toney.

Dec. 18, 1819   Burton, William, and Sarah Clarke.

Dec. 17, 1823   Bush, Henry, and Sarah George.

Apr. 7, 1820   Byington, Moses (of Franklin County), and Cythia Cheely, consent of Cuthbert and Elizabeth Cheely.

Jan. 11, 1813   Byrd, Mason, and Silvey Thacker.

Nov. 30, 1801   Cahall, Edward, and Elizabeth Hughes, dau. of Rees Hughes.

Jan. 28, 1817   Cahill, Peregrin, and Anna Pyrtle.

Jan. 13, 1821   Callaway, John, and America Hairston, dau. of George Hairston.

Dec. 31, 1840   Carter, Cary (of Franklin County), and Elizabeth Dillon, consent of Elisor Dillon.

Mar. 31, 1846   Carter, Cary, and Elvira Duvall.

May 10, 1814   Carter, Edward, and Nancy Allen.

July 13, 1846   Carter, Fleming, and Martha Philpott.

Jan. 26, 1836   Carter, George, and Elizabeth Odle, consent of James and Nellie Odle.

Mar. 15, 1814   Carter, Harriss, and Mary Dillen.

May 25, 1795   Carter, Jessee, and Elizabeth Phillpot, consent of John and Mary Ann Philpot.

Oct. 5, 1812   Carter, John, and Nancy Philpott.

June 24, 1778   Carter, Joseph, and Nancy Menefee, dau. of William Menefee.

Jan. 16, 1794   Carter, Joseph, and Mary Dillion.

Mar. 29, 1831   Carter, Dr. William, and Sarah Ann Morris, consent of Benj. S. Morris.

May 26, 1800   Cary, William, and Salley Lyle, consent only of James Lyle.

Dec. 29, 1828   Casey, Thomas, and Sally Rice.

Apr. 27, 1793   Cason, Edward, and Lucy Edwards.

Jan. 20, 1827   Cayton, Martin, son of C. Cayton, and Nancy Pullom, dau. of William Pulliam.

Jan, 4, 1793   Cayton, William, and Rachel Oakes, dau of John Oakes.

July 4, 1808   Cheatham, Edmund, and Francinia Bouldin, dau. of Joseph Bouldin.

Jan. 13, 1844   Cheatham, Edmund B., and Rachel Ann Gravely,
                    dau. of Lewis Gravely.

Nov. 20, 1804   Cheatham, Leonard, Jr., and Jeaney Dillard, dau.
                    of John Dillard.

Sept. 19, 1838   Cheatham, Peter D., and Mary A. Spencer, dau. of
                    Ruth Spencer.

Nov. 22, 1804   Cheatham, Thomas, and ----- ----

Oct. 8, 1838   Cheeley, Cuthbert, and Catharine M. Dickerson, dau. of
                    Jemima Dickerson.

Dec. 15, 1830   Cheeley, William, and Marion G. Rowland, step-dau.
                    of William Potter.

Dec. 11, 1811   Cheely, Cuthburth, and Elizabeth Northcutt.

Jan. 17, 1844   Chesher, James, and Frances Self.

Oct. 23, 1833   Cheshier, Thomas, and Elizabeth A. Minter, dau.
                    of Othniel Minter.

July 18, 1837   Chessure, Coleman, and Mary Land.

Dec. 10, 1838   Chessure, Daniel, and Elizabeth Rowland, granddau.
                    of Mathew Seay, Sr.

Sept. 9, 1846   Childress, John, ad Martha Barker.

Apr. 26, 1778   Chowning, John, and Lettice Payne, dau. of John Payne.

Jan. 29, 1802   Christian, Capt. John, and Elizabeth Dillard, dau. of
                    John Dillard.

Nov. 4, 1779   Clack, John, and Sally Standifer, dau. of James
                    Standifer.

June 26, 1813   Clanton, Macklan, and Winny Oldham, dau. of
                    Elizabeth Oldham.

July 25, 1842   Clark, Absalom, and Malinda Mills.

Sept. 23, 1838   Clark, Gideon, and Cassandra B. Stultz.

Aug. 22, 1801   Clark, Henry, and Casandra Phillpot, dau. of
                    Charles Phillpot.

Jan. 2, 1817   Clark, James, and Mourning Martin.

Apr. 14, 1828   Clark, John, and Henrietta Clark.

Jan. 2, 1813   Clark, Jonathan, and Patsy Hensly.

Dec. 12, 1828   Clark, William, and Ann Martin, dau. of Stephen Martin.

Jan. 6, 1826   Clark, Willis, and Edda Martin, dau. of Stephen
Martin.

Sept. 12, 1820   Clarke, Isaac, and Susannah Gravely.

Dec. 18, 1842   Clarke, John, Jr., and Jane Clark, dau. of J-(?) C. Clark.

Dec. 11, 1820   Clarke, Thomas, and Sally Carver.

Mar. 29, 1826   Clarke, William H., and Casandra A. Marshall, consent
of Dennis Marshall.

Nov. 25, 1843   Clemons, John, and Mary S. Clift, dau. of William
and Susannah Clift.

Nov. 5, 1817   Clift, William, and Susannah Hankins.

July 19, 1828   Clinkscales, James, and Jennett Dillard, dau. of
George Dillard.

Nov. 24, 1804   Clinton, Henry, and Mary Spencer.

Jan. 8, 1844   Clowers, George W., and Susan Davis.

Mar. 13, 1826   Cobb, Nelson, and Mary Gilley.

---- -- 1827   Cobler, John, and Sally Bouldin.

Aug. 5, 1780   Cockram, Wm., and Salley Edmundson.

Mar. 28, 1808   Cole, Samuel M., and Keturiah Miller.

Nov. 21, 1836   Coleman, James, and Caleniece Feazle, dau. of
Aaron Feazle.

Oct. 17, 1780   Colley, John, and Sarah France, dau. of Henry France.

Mar. 30, 1795   Compton, Arthemus, and Elizabeth Crowley. Frankey
Crowley makes affidavit that "parents are willing."

May 6, 1894   Compton, Evenazer, and Ailcey Hopper, dau. of
Thomas and Mymah Hopper.

Jan. 5, 1842   Compton, James, and Martha Eggleton.

Dec. 5, 1827   Connaway, Robert, and Tabithia Deshazo, dau. of
William Deshazo.

Oct. 13, 1817   Conway, Benjm., and Martha Harper Marshall,
dau. of Dennis Marshall.

Nov. 5, 1782   Conway, John, and Elizabeth Williams, dau. of
John Williams, dec'd.

Apr. 27, 1795   Cook, Alexander, and Ann Dillion. James Cook, Sr. "paid fee for license."

Sept. 30, 1828   Cook, Major Robert, and Susan Martin.

June 7, 1814   Cooksey, Edmund, and Fanny Reed.

Oct. 28, 1830   Cooper, Alexander, and Mary Nunn.

July 5, 1803   Cooper, Elisha, and Polley Taylor.

Aug. 24, 1837   Cooper, Greensville, and Sally T. Altick.

June 10, 1828   Cooper, Hubert, and Sally L. King, dau. of Mary King.

Jan. 6, 1837   Cormick, Capt. Lewis M., and Mary Perkins, dau. of Wm. Perkins.

July 2, 1807   Corsey, Charles, and Susanna Toombs.

Feb. 26, 1822   Cousins, Francis M., and Lucinda Norman, Thos. Shelton, grdn. for wife.

Dec. 28, 1849   Cousins, Henry M., and America Cousins.

Dec. 10, 1839   Covington, John, and Sarah Pulliam, dau. of William Pulliam.

May 3, 1819   Covington, William, and Mary Larrison.

Sept. 27, 1823   Cox, Bennett, and Patsy Gilly.

Sept. 6, 1791   Cox, John, and Leanner Bolling.

Apr. 28, 1829   Cox, John, and Elizabeth Cox, dau. of Rachel Cox.

Feb. 24, 1806   Cox, Larkin, and Nancey Rea.

Aug. 11, 1828   Cox, Peter C., and Mary Ann Harris, dau. of Lucy Harris.

Jan. 13, 1795   Cox, Thomas, and Lucy Watson, consent of William Watson.

Jan. 11, 1820   Cox, William, and Nancy Gilly.

Dec. 24, 1833   Cox, William K., and Manurvey Cayton, dau. of Cornelius Cayton.

Oct. 14, 1846   Craghead, Thomas L., and Lucinda T. Baker, dau. of Catharine Baker.

June 26, 1797   Craig, Thomas, and Mary Davis.

Dec. 9, 1841	Craig, William, and Salley Oakley.
Dec. 31, 1798	Crane, Samuel, and Elizabeth Delozer.
May 12, 1841	Creasey, Henry, son of John Creasey, and Nancy Barker, dau. of Joseph Barker.
Feb. 26, 1810	Creasey, Joseph, and Delilah Jones, consent of Henry Jones.
Oct. 27, 1836	Creasy, James, and Virginia Norman, dau. of Dutton Norman.
Mar. 13, 1815	Creasy, William, and Elizabeth Bateman.
Apr. 11, 1831	Crews, Gideon, and Eliza C. Bouldin.
Aug. 18, 1830	Crews, Samuel, and Marial Hatcher, dau. of A. Hatcher.
Feb. 25, 1837	Critenden, James, and Eliza R. Grant, consent of Archibald and Lydia Grant.
Feb. 20, 1778	Crouch, Joseph, and Peggy Sandford, dau. of George Sandford.
July 8, 1845	Crouch, Woodson, and Salenia Ann Wilson.
July 16, 1793	Cunningham, Jos., and Nancy Dains (?).
Nov. 27, 1793	Cunningham, William, and Mary Pyrtle.
Dec. 27, 1837	Curry, William, and Harriet Pullium, dau. of Drury Pullium.
Dec. 24, 1821	Curtis, Elisha B., and Bethena H. Jackson.
Aug. 28, 1826	Dakin, Preston, and Caroline Stacy, dau. of Elizabeth Stacy.
Aug. 13, 1832	Dallas, Bird, and Susanna E. Crews, consent of John Crews.
Nov. 25, 1845	Dalton, John A. B. (of Stokes County, N. C.), and Martha A. Mathews, dau. of James Mathews.
July 13, 1798	Dandridge, Nathaniel West, Jr., and Martha Fontaine. M. Fontaine, grdn. and parent of wife.
May 29, 1819	Dandridge, Thomas B., and Caroline Matilda Nicholds.
Jan. 26, 1807	Daniel, John, and Venia (?) Wilson.
Sept. 28, 1844	Daulton, James, and Mary Jane Eanes, dau. of Arthur W. Eanes.

May 1, 1826	Daulton, William, and Polly Jones, consent of Charles Jones.
Dec. 14, 1800	Davies, Benjamin, and Nancy Heard, dau. of Wm. Heard.
Sept. 22, 1845	Davis, Benjamin, and Elizabeth M. Hix.
Jan. 8, 1838	Davis, Brice, and Nancy Lane.
Nov. 28, 1836	Davis, Coleman, and Nancy Chessure.
May 19, 1814	Davis, George, and Lettice Wyatt, "Over 21 years of age."
Sept. 5, 1829	Davis, Israel, and Rachel Gilley, consent of George and Surina Gilly.
Sept. 11, 1809	Davis, John, and Patsey Williams, dau. of William Williams.
Jan. 1, 1824	Davis, Patrick H., and Mary H. Taylor.
Dec. 6, 1807	Davis, Peter, and Mary Heard.
Nov. 3, 1806	Davis, Robert, and Joanna Hewlett, dau. of Wm. Hewlett.
Feb. 29, 1808	Davis, Robert, and Mary Roberts.
Apr. 8, 1797	Davis, Samuel, and Charity King, dau. of John King.
Nov. 28, 1839	Davis, Thomas B., and Martha Coleman.
Nov. 11, 1812	Davis, William, Jr., and Phebe Creacy (?).
May 13, 1825	Davis, William, and Elizabeth McBride.
Jan. 19, 1795	Davis, Williamson, and Elenor Davis.
July 6, 1807	Davis, Williamson, and Jean Morris (or Norris).
May 24, 1827	Dawson, John, and Elizabeth Peddigo, dau. of Elijah Peddigo.
Oct. 20, 1832	Dearin, James, and Ann C. Toler. A. Toler (for wife).
Nov. 28, 1803	Degraffenreid, Francis, and Tabitha King.
Oct. 7, 1829	Delozier, Perin, son of Edward Delozier, and Franciana Minter, dau. of Othniel and Joice Minter.
Dec. 17, 1811	Dent, Benjamin, and Nancy Shackleford.
Nov. 16, 1783	Dent, Shadrick, and Mary Murphy, dau. of James Murphy

July 20, 1811   Deshaure, Elizah, and Eliza. Jarviss.

Apr. 13, 1828   Deshazo, Richard, and Elizabeth Allen.

June 2, 1781   Dickerson, John, and Isbell Woods.

Dec. 28, 1795   Dickson, Jeremiah, and Lucy Jones.

Jan. 27, 1803   Dillard, George S., and Patsy Hill.

Jan. 8, 1846   Dillard, John H. (of Patrick Co.), and Ann Martin, dau. of Jos. Martin.

Feb. 6, 1843   Dillard, Overton R., and Sally Martin, dau. of Jos. Martin.

May 29, 1819   Dillard, Peter H., and Eliza. W. Redd.

Jan. 20, 1845   Dillard, Dr. Peter F., and Elizabeth Hairston. Samuel Hairston, grdn. of wife.

Mar. 19, 1792   Dillen, Benjamin, Jr., and Elizabeth Witty, consent only.

July 12, 1804   Dillen, James, and Elizabeth Meredith.

Sept. 26, 1824   Dillen, Jefferson, and Sarah Pace.

Dec. 19, 1792   Dillen, William, Jr., and Tabitha Witt.

Sept. 12, 1825   Dillen, William, and Elizabeth Nunn.

July 19, 1793   Dilliner, Henry, and Lucy Murphy.

Mar. 2, 1792   Dillingham, Lott, and Ann Dillingham.

Jan. 19, 1808   Dillion, William, and Sally Pigg, dau. of James Pigg.

Feb. 16, 1839   Dillon, Elison, and Delila Carter, dau. of Cairy and Mahala Carter.

Nov. - 1829   Dillon, William, and Susan Lanier, dau. of Benjamin Lanier, consent only.

Oct. 8, 1804   Dix, Thomas, and Lucy Miller.

Dec. 8, 1845   Dodson, Josiah, and Jane Bray.

Aug. 3, 1846   Doland, Charles, and Catharine Sams, dau. of William Sams.

Apr. 13, 1779   Dooley, Thomas, and Lucy Webb.

Aug. 11, 1831   Doss, John, and Catharine Philips, "21 years of age", dau. of Susannah Philips.

Jan. 11, 1807   Doss, Noah, and Lucy Pyrtle.

Sept. 2, 1795   Dougherty, Samuel, and Mary Lovin.

Feb. 24, 1837   Doyle, William M., and Elizabeth Minter, dau. of
Silas Minter.

Feb. 26, 1810   Draper, John, and Ruth Clark.

Sept. 22, 1845   Draper, John W., and Mary Jane Turner.

Dec. 18, 1827   Draper, Thomas, and Nancy Davis.

Sept. 30, 1805   Draper, William, and Lucy Meredith.

May 23, 1835   Draper, William, and Lucy Draper.

Dec. 18, 1845   Draper, William F., and Mary Goode, dau. of
Samuel Goode.

Mar. 9, 1812   Duncan, Archibald, and Nancy Vaughan.

Feb. 10, 1845   Dunigan, Thomas E., and Eleanor Gravely, dau. of
Lewis Gravely.

Dec. 23, 1843   Dunivant, James, and Rebecca Mills, dau. of James B.
and Catharine Mills.

Nov. 24, 1800   Dunn, Hezekiah, and Molley Wilson.

Feb. 10, 1845   Dunn, James D., and Anne Lewis.

Jan. 15, 1796   Durham, William, and Susanah Hatcher.

Feb. 22, 1823   Duvall, Marine, and Jane Bauldin.

July 4, 1801   Dyer, Benjamin, and Polley Gravely.

Feb. 25, 1810   Dyer, David, and Nancy Salmon, consent of
Mary Salmon.

Jan. 10, 1831   Dyer, Fontaine, and Harriett Cheeley, dau. of
Cuthbert Cheeley,

Oct. 29, 1825   Dyer, George, and Margaret Spencer.

Oct. 2, 1834   Dyer, George, and Nancy George.

Mar. 1, 1833   Dyer, Hugh, and Ruth Draper, dau. of William Draper.

July 16, 1798   Dyer, James, and Sarah Ann Fortune.

July 23, 1823   Dyer, Jefferson, and Margaret Salmon, dau. of
John Salmon.

Aug. 10, 1829   Dyer, Jefferson, and Elizabeth Custer.

Nov. 27, 1824	Dyer, Joab, and Mary Salmon, dau. of John Salmon.
July 10, 1837	Dyer, Joab, and Nancy Drucilla Harvey.
Apr. 8, 1811	Dyer, Joel, and Polly Salmon.
May 1, 1827	Dyer, Joel, consent of Jesse Dyer, and Isbell Barker, dau. of Joseph Barker.
Nov. 10, 1838	Dyer, John S., consent of D. Dyer, and Martha Bassett, dau. of Alexander Bassett.
Oct. 4, 1797	Eadens, John, and Polly Masters.
June 18, 1792	Earles, Joshua, and Elizabeth Lucas, dau. of Mary Lucas.
Sept. 24, 1804	Earls, Thomas, and Sarah Arthur.
Nov. 30, 1816	East, John, and Elizabeth Payne, dau. of Reuban Payne.
June 15, 1795	East, Joseph, and Jinney Rea, dau. of James Rea.
Nov. 19, 1816	East, Joseph, and Mildred Payne.
Jan. 26, 1802	East, William, and Elizabeth Thurston.
Feb. 23, 1807	East, William, and Salley Webb.
Nov. 28, 1825	Easter (or Esther), Wiley, son of Martha Esther, and Margaret Mullins.
Nov. 6, 1835	Eaton, Daniel, and Tabitha W. Bradberry.
Nov. 22, 1779	Edmundson, Humphrey, and Frances Swanson, dau. of William Swanson.
Dec. 15, 1823	Edwards, Chiles, and Nancy D. Hewlett.
June 10, 1814	Edwards, Henry, and Sarah Matilda Waller, dau. of Carr Waller.
Mar. 17, 1812	Edwards, James, and Polly McMillion.
Sept. 24, 1849	Edwards, James M., and Elizabeth Good, dau. of Samuel Good.
Sept. 26, 1807	Edwards, John, and Martha Johnson.
Oct. 29, 1794	Edwards, Owen, and Judith Morton, dau. of James Morton.
Aug. 7, 1849	Edwards, Stephen, and Elizabeth Mary Dillion.

Aug. 2, 1791   Edwards, William, and Elizabeth Brittain, consent of George Brittain.

Aug. 29, 1840   Edwards, Williamson K., and Jane Bowles.

Sept. 4, 1826   Egelton, Thomas, and Dosha Pace.

Mar. 9, 1829   Eggleton, Joseph, and Chaney Wyatt.

Oct. 29, 1828   Eggleton, Michael, and Eliza F. Robertson.

Nov. 18, 1841   Eggleton, Nathaniel, and Delila Stultz, dau. of Thomas Stultz.

Dec. 22, 1817   Egleton, George, and Nancy Bouldin.

June 18, 1804   Egleton, Thomas, and Polley Fleemon.

Apr. 6, 1793   Elkins, David, and Mary Pedigoe, consent of Robert Pedigoe.

Apr. 23, 1795   Elkins, James, and Leah Vintson.

Sept. 7, 1844   Ellington, James D., and Wilmoth H. Stone, dau. of Seffereign Stone.

Oct. 29, 1798   Elliott, Joseph, and Prudence Crawley.

Dec. 8, 1817   Elston, James, and Zilpha Gunn.

Oct. 21, 1822   Estes, Jesse, and Maria Fortune.

Mar. 23, 1796   Evans, James, and Milley Oakley, dau. of Thomas Oakley.

Nov. 7, 1849   Fagg, Charles, and Sally Ann Stone, dau. of James Stone.

Dec. 20, 1814   Faris, Daniel, and Nancy Smith.

Nov. 23, 1844   Faris, George W., and Adeline Bryant, dau. of James Bryant.

June 26, 1836   Fariss, William W., and Nancy Minter.

Aug. 1, 1807   Farris, Archibald, and Anna Leake.

Dec. 16, 1817   Farris, Coleman, and Elizabeth West, dau. of Nicholas West.

Nov. 8, 1819   Farris, Harrison, and Sarah Rea.

Jan. 6, 1792   Farris, Thomas, and Judith Quarles, dau. of David Quarles.

Feb. 8, 1823   Farriss, Archabald, Jr., and Nancy Farriss.

Sept. 18, 1834   Feazel, John M., and Mary Coleman.

May 16, 1836   Feazle, Joab, and Jane Nunn, dau. of Levinia Nunn.

May 15, 1798   Fee, Henry, and Nelly Long.

Jan. 9, 1815   Fernenho, Milton, and Martha M. Edwards, dau. of
Ambrose Edwards.

Apr. 11, 1803   Fifer (or Phifer), Bradley, and Polley Hibbert,
"19 years of age."

Nov. 14, 1819   Fields, Nathaniel, and Nancy H. Scales.

Feb. 13, 1832   Finney, John, and Frances King, dau. of Mary King.

Feb. 12, 1849   Finney, Joshua, and Caroline Staples.

Feb. 2, 1810   Fishback, William, and Pamelia A. Johnson, consent
of Benjamin and Frances Johnson.

Dec. 1, 1849   Flanagan, Burwell, and Martha Odle, dau. of
James and Nelly Odel.

Nov. 9, 1840   Flanigan, Beverly (alias Price), son of Thomas Price,
and Nancy Odle, dau. of James Odell.

June 30, 1818   Fleeman, George, and Patsy Perkinson.

Apr. 9, 1839   Fleeman, Hezekiah, son of George Fleeman, and Ethney
Malinda Carter, dau. of Phillip and Saly Carter.

Mar. 27, 1809   Fleeman, John, and Elizabeth Griffin, dau. of
Griffith Griffin.

Jan. 18, 1820   Fleeman, Thomas, and Sarah Thomason, dau. of
Peter and Elizabeth Thomason.

Dec. 22, 1842   Fleemon, Joseph, and Kezia Mathews, dau. of Luke Mathews.

Feb. 22, 1832   Fleming, Hodges, and Mary Hodges. John and Rebecca
Hodges, consent for both.

Sept. 29, 1828   Floyd, Benjamin H., and Malinda Moore, dau. of
James Moore.

Aug. 12, 1828   Floyd, William P., and Jane S. Mills.

July 25, 1849   Fontaine, Charles H., and Martha C. Nowlin, dau. of
B. W. Nowlin.

Jan. 23, 1797   Fontaine, Patrick H., and Nancy Miller.

Sept. 25, 1832   Fontaine, Patrick Henry, Jr., and Sarah Cole.

Sept. 12, 1836   Forbes, Austin, and Nancy East.

June 30, 1840   Forbes, John R., and Nancy L. Agee.

Aug. 1, 1800   Ford, Andrew, and Nancy Jones.

Feb. 13, 1809   Fortune, Joseph, and Lucy Shackleford, dau. of John
Shackleford, consent only.

Feb. 8, 1813   Foster, James, and Dosha Burgess.

Nov. 9, 1809   Foster, John, and Elizabeth Foster.

Sept. 11, 1837   Fowler, William, and Elizabeth East, dau. of William
East, Sr.

Apr. 16, 1836   Francis, Matthew, and Mary Allen.

Nov. 24, 1835   Franklin, George, and Jane G. ------

July 24, 1837   Fretwell, William, and Mary J. Norman.

Oct. 29, 1845   Fry, Archilus, and (Martha Mills).

May 18, 1824   Fulkerson, Frederick, and Mary Rea.

Feb. 29, 1780   Fuller, Brittain, and Nancy Jackson.

Mar. 5, 1832   Galloway, James S., and Elizabeth B. Morrison, consent
of George Morrison.

Nov. 14, 1807   Garner, Thomas, and Fanny Warren.

Jan. 19, 1808   Garner, William, and Nancy Davis.

Dec. 23, 1835   Garrett, William, and Jane Watson, dau. of Stinson Watson.

Dec. 17, 1845   Garrot, John, and Susan E. Bradley.

Nov. 9, 1798   Garrott, Gideon, and Lucy Morris, consent of Mary Morris.

Jan. 12, 1829   Garthart, John, and Polly Pergusson.

Oct. 16, 1810   Gaulding, Moses, and Susanna Elliott.

Dec. 23, 1831   Gear, Reubin, and Casah Meredith, dau. of
Greenville Meredith.

Oct. 30, 1798   Gearhart, Peter, and Obedience Alexander.

Aug. 3, 1813   Gessett, Cavin, and Polly Fifer.

Feb. 10, 1840   Gilley, Alfred, and Harriet Cayton, consent of Cornelius Cayton.

Jan. 14, 1814	Gilley, Benjm., and Mary Wilson.
Feb. 17, 1835	Gilley, Benjamin, and Nancy Stratton.
July 24, 1840	Gilley, Burwell, and Salley Gilley.
Nov. 30, 1816	Gilley, Francis, and Lucy Kelly, dau. of John Cally.
July 29, 1819	Gilley, Francis, and Polly Hewlett, dau. of William Hewlett.
Mar. 19, 1813	Gilley, George, and Lavina Wilson.
Dec. 12, 1849	Gilley, James M., and Jane Wilson.
Jan. 5, 1801	Gilley, Joseph, and Elizabeth Briant.
Apr. 3, 1843	Gilley, Joseph, and Mary G. Hopper.
Mar. - 1845	Gilley, Joseph, and Elizabeth Stratton.
Feb. 1, 1842	Gilley, Leftwich, "not of lawful age," consent of Peter Gilley, and Mary Gilley, consent of Benjamin Gilley.
Jan. 11, 1819	Gilley, Peter, and One (?) Murfry, dau. of William Murfry.
Jan. 5, 1841	Gilley, Samuel, and Martha Cox.
Apr. 8, 1822	Gilley, William, and Mary Gilley.
Dec. 10, 1808	Gilliam, John B., and Jean Anthony.
Feb. 21, 1842	Glass, Armistead W., and Eliza Taylor, dau. of Zilly Taylor.
Dec. 8, 1810	Glass, Benjm., and Susannah Franklyn.
Jan. 3, 1813	Glass, James, and Sally Shackleford, dau. of William Shackleford.
Sept. 2, 1801	Going, Simeon, and Keziah Tabb.
Nov. 30, 1821	Golden, Andy, and Unity Bray.
July 31, 1830	Goode, Thomas, and Coley Barber.
Sept. 15, 1819	Goodman, William, and Mary Wilson.
Oct. 13, 1825	Goodman, David, and Agnes Harris.
Nov. 3, 1800	Goodwin, Joseph, and Polly Oakes.
Apr. 15, 1805	Goolsby, Charles, and Armine Anglin, dau. of Phillip Anglin.

Nov. 28, 1838   Gouldin, Wesley, and Mary Taylor, dau. of Zillar Taylor. Jno. Dillard, grdn. of wife.

Oct. 27, 1794   Gover, William, and Sarah Griggs.

Nov. 20, 1846   Grant, John H., and Pocahontas Dickinson, dau. of Catharine M. Cheely.

Jan. 24, 1826   Graveley, John, and Winefred Shumate.

May 13, 1816   Graveley, Joseph, and Polly Higgs.

Dec. 11, 1845   Gravely, Benjamin F., and Julia C. Thomas, dau. of Nancy Thomas.

Aug. 14, 1843   Gravely, Booker, and Edey Mathews.

Feb. 14, 1826   Gravely, George, and Mary M. Hughes.

Oct. 31, 1842   Gravely, George, son of Jos. Gravely, and Lucinda Cooper.

Nov. 9, 1825   Gravely, Edmond, and Susan Robertson.

Jan. 12, 1835   Gravely, Jabez L., and Martha L. Hankins, dau. of William Hankins.

Mar. 27, 1797   Gravely, Jabez, and Judith Wills, dau. of John Wills.

Jan. 10, 1842   Gravely, John K., and Mary G. Clanton.

Dec. 30, 1799   Gravely, Joseph, and Helen King.

Nov. 9, 1846   Gravely, Peyton, and Martha Ann Wingfield.

Dec. 16, 1800   Graves, Thomas, and Elizabeth Lanier, consent of David Lanier.

Dec. 3, 1836   Gravley, George, and Matilda Clark, dau. of John Clark.

Feb. 8, 1831   Gravley, William, and Lidia Clark, consent of John Clark.

June 10, 1823   Gravly, Joseph K., and Permelia Stults.

Dec. 19, 1822   Gravly, Lewis, and Martha Dyer, dau. of George Dyer.

Dec. 20, 1824   Gravly, Willis, and Dolly Stone.

Sept. 14, 1818   Gray, Thomas, and Nancy Harris.

Mar. 25, 1805   Gray, William, and Rachel Wade.

Apr. 25, 1785   Grayham, Arthur, and Elizabeth Batty (?).

Sept. 22, 1806	Green, James, and Salley Harris.
Mar. 4, 1811	Greenlee, David, and Martha Hunter.
Dec. 31, 1806	Greenlee, Ephriam, M., and Salley Hord, grdn. James Greenlee.
Sept. 18, 1804	Greenlee, James, and Ruth Hord.
Jan. 18, 1832	Gregory, John, and Susan King, dau. of Joseph S. King.
Mar. 15, 1839	Gregory, William, and Lucy Dillion, dau. of Elizabeth Dillion.
Dec. 23, 1843	Gregory, William, and Eliza Jones, dau. of Dorcas Jones.
July 25, 1782	Griffith, William, and Susannah Jones, dau. of Thomas Jones.
Sept. 4, 1822	Grigg, Joseph W., and Delilah McCullough, dau. of James McCullough.
July 15, 1836	Griggs, George, and Frances Wills, dau. of Thomas Wills.
Nov. 9, 1836	Griggs, Ira, and Sally King.
July 30, 1792	Griggs, John, and Phebe Acholas (?)
Nov. 9, 1846	Griggs, John G., and Sarah F. Stults, dau. of Adam Stults.
Nov. 30, 1799	Griggs, Michael, and Betsey Minter, dau. of John Minter.
Apr. 7, 1804	Griggs, Michael, and Caty Stults.
June 4, 1817	Griggs, Michael, and Patsey Perkinson.
Nov. 18, 1820	Griggs, Michael, and Sally Peddigo, dau. of Joseph Pedigo.
Apr. 11, 1836	Griggs, Peter, and Lucy Gilley.
Dec. 10, 1836	Griggs, Peter F., and Dorotha Clanton.
Sept. 10, 1838	Griggs, Wesley, and Susan W. King, dau. of Susan King.
Apr. 11, 1821	Grogan, Francis, and Nancy Stone, dau. of John Stone.
Feb. 27, 1832	Grogan, Francis, and Elizabeth Hopper.
Jan. 10, 1825	Grogan, Richard, and Elizabeth Stone.

June 29, 1801	Gunn, Elisha, and Salley Smith, consent of John Smith.
Apr. 14, 1827	Gyer, Joseph, and Susan Dillion.
Sept. 10, 1844	Hagood, Anderson M., and Mary B. Marshall, dau. of Benj. A. Marshall.
Dec. 3, 1803	Hailey, Barnaba, and Nancy Coursey.
Apr. 27, 1816	Hailey, Edward, and Mary Thomasson.
Feb. 27, 1823	Haily, Gabriel, son of Thomas Haily, and Delila Minter, dau. of Othniel Minter.
Dec. 10, 1827	Haily, James, and Sidney Meredith.
May 6, 1837	Hairfield, David J., and Elizabeth ------
July 14, 1837	Hairston, George S., and Matilda M. Martin, dau. of Jos. Martin.
June 1, 1808	Hairston, Hardin, and Sally S. Staples, dau. of John Staples.
May 22, 1843	Hairston, Nicholas H., and Sarah S. Dillard, dau. of Jno. Dillard.
Mar. 3, 1827	Hairston, Peter, and Ruth Hairston.
July 8, 1833	Haley, Benjamin, and Mahaley Shumate.
Jan. 9, 1815	Haley, Tavner, and Joyce Thomason, dau. of Peter Thomason.
Dec. 20, 1792	Haley, William, and Nancy Jackson, dau. of Daniel Jackson.
Dec. 21, 1824	Hall, John, and Temperance Hankins.
Oct. 13, 1835	Hamlett, William J., and Martha A. W. Thomas, dau. of Nancy Thomas.
Apr. 18, 1783	Hamilton, George, and Agnes Cooper.
Jan. 6, 1794	Hampton, Laban, and Leany Stephens, consent of Williams Stephens.
Feb. 7, 1810	Hanby, William, and Sarah Waller.
Feb. 14, 1834	Hanes, Isaac N., "22 years old," and Ann Stone.
Jan. 24, 1825	Haney, Lewis, and Ann Cobb.
Jan. 22, 1842	Hankins, James A., and Elizabeth Jane Barrow, consent of Jesse (?) Barrow.

Oct. 16, 1793   Hannah, Alexander, and Sarah Pelphry, consent of
                 John and Elizabeth Pelphry.

June 16, 1804   Hannah, Townley, and Elizabeth Bellama.

Dec. 26, 1803   Harbour, John, and Jean Moore.

July 31, 1799   Hardeman, Constant, and Sally J. Marr.

Feb. 5, 1893   Hardy, Charles, and Rachel Parsley.

Dec. 30, 1831   Hardy, Curtis, and Mary Bocock.

May 24, 1827   Hardy, John, and Sarah Peddigo, dau. of Elijah Peddigo.

Apr. 3, 1830   Hardy, Joseph, and Nancy Pace.

Nov. 19, 1805   Hardy, Owen, and Sarah Hibbert, dau. of Charles Hibbert.

Jan. 31, 1816   Hardy, Thrashley, and Francis Daniel.

Dec. 18, 1838   Hardy, Thrashly, and Polly Hensley, consent of Unity Hensley.

June 11, 1827   Harris, Daniel, and Jane Wilson, dau. of Thomas Wilson.

Jan. 1, 1821   Harris, Fuler, and Sarah Bateman.

Oct. 8, 1829   Harris, Henry, and Elizabeth Bishop, dau. of
                 Landon J. Bishop.

Jan. 25, 1826   Harris, James, and Louisianna Jones, consent of
                 Thomas Jones.

Sept. 28, 1821   Harris, Joseph, and Elizabeth Hill.

Jan. 25, 1802   Harriss, Moses, and Dorciss Stephens.

Nov. 20, 1834   Harvell, Merritt, and Tabitha Minter, consent of
                 Othneil Minter.

Nov. 30, 1807   Harvil, Marcus, and Winney Thomason.

Nov. 22, 1849   Harville, George A., and Mary A. Barker, dau. of
                 James Barker.

Oct. 22, 1807   Hatcher, Archd., Jr., and Nancy Shelton.

Oct. 1, 1778   Hawkins, Benjamin, and Molly Taylor, dau. of
                 William Taylor.

Oct. 30, 1798   Hays, William, Jr., and Elizabeth Wade.

Aug. 12, 1809   Heard, William, and Elizabeth Rowland.

Mar. 9, 1826	Heard, William, and Mary Meredith, consent of Elijah Meredith.
Feb. 25, 1842	Hefflefinger, Greenville, and Nancy Cooper.
Feb. 22, 1839	Heffelfinger, Henry, and Catharine Powers, alias Haffelfinger.
Dec. 11, 1815	Hefflinger, Jacob, and Elizabeth Burgess.
Nov. 28, 1804	Hemming, William, and Delilah McKinzey.
March 29, 1812	Hensley, John, and Nancy Salmon.
Oct. 1, 1845	Hensley, William, and Frances Ann Bocock.
Sept. 17, 1817	Hereford, John L., and Jemima Ramy.
Nov. 10, 1823	Hereford, Josiah, and Martha Staples, dau. of Norman Staples.
Apr. 23, 1817	Hereford, Dr. William, and Eliza. Ann Dandridge, dau. of N. W. Dandridge.
Apr. 9, 1803	Hewlett, John, and Polly Payne, dau. of Reuben Payne.
Jan. 8, 1812	Hibbert, William, and Lucy Munroe.
June 28, 1826	Hickman, Benjamin T., son of Edwin Hickman (of Stokes Co., N. C.), and Judith F. Christian, dau. of Jno. Christian.
Dec. 13, 1819	Hicks, Thomas C., and Nelly Stults.
Jan. 4, 1849	Higgs, Samuel, and Lavinia McDaniel (or McDonalld), consent of John McDonalld.
Apr. 11, 1825	Higgs, William, and Nancy Chessure.
--- 10, 1784	Hill, Amannuel, and Mary Fulkerson; consent only, Mary and Frederick Fulkerson, consent for wife.
June 20, 1816	Hill, Jno. W., and Judia Hill.
Nov. 25, 1826	Hill, Manning, and Elizabeth Letcher Gunnell, dau. of James G. Gunnell.
Feb. 16, 1836	Hill, Robert S., and Mary Lanier, dau. of Benjamin Lanier.
May 13, 1805	Hill, Thomas, and Lucindy Payne, dau. of Reuben Payne.
Nov. 17, 1840	Hill, William W., grdn, J. Hamlett, and Mary Catharine Bassett, dau. of Alexander H. Bassett.

Aug. 12, 1844   Hix, William N., and Judith N. Gravely.

Jan. 28, 1839   Hodges, John, and Fidilia Clark.

Sept. 14, 1829   Hodges, Obediah, and Betsey Fleeman.

Jan. 19, 1780   Hogans, Wm., and Nancy Dillard, dau. of James Dillard.

July 20, 1812   Holland, Stephen, and Lucy Davis.

Sept. 2, 1844   Holland, William, and Sarah W. Norman, consent of Dutten Norman.

Dec. 3, 1820   Hollandsworth, Brice, and Ann Garrett Philpott, dau. of Charles Philpott.

Dec. 1, 1823   Hollandsworth, Thomas, and Mary Nunn.

Dec. 30, 1815   Holt, Harod, and Martha Salmon.

Dec. 9, 1822   Holt, Pascal, and Rachel Jones.

Apr. 25, 1835   Holloway, John H., and ---- ----

Nov. 16, 1842   Hopper, Allen, and Eliza Bassett, dau. of Alexander Bassett.

Sept. 20, 1823   Hopper, Ezekiah, and Mildred F. Hill, dau. of Maning Hill.

June 15, 1821   Hopper, James, and Elizabeth Bays.

July 30, 1822   Hopper, John, and Jane Lemon.

Feb. 2, 1814   Hopper, Terrell, and Rhody Lane, dau. of Mary Lane.

May 18, 1793   Hopper, William, and Hester Stevens (or Susannah Stephens), consent of William Stevens.

Sept. 1, 1828   Houston, David G., and Ann Dix.

Mar. 26, 1804   Howard, James, and Nancy King.

July 25, 1835   Hubbard, Moses, and Martha Watkins.

Nov. 8, 1819   Hudson, Daniel, and Sophia Clinkscales.

Jan. 25, 1802   Hughes, Micajah, and Lettice Reamey, dau. of Daniel Reamey.

Mar. 7, 1812   Hughes, Ruben, and Polly Martin.

Nov. 1, 1796   Hughes, Terry, and Jemima Reamy.

Oct. 25, 1828   Hughs, Madison R., and Sarah S. Dillard.

July 17, 1805	Humphreys, Morriss, Jr., and Disey Long, sister of Reuben Long.
Oct. 21, 1844	Hundley, Ambrose D., and Susan C. Devin, dau. of James Devin.
Jan. 2, 1824	Hundley, George, son of John Hundley, and Emblem M. Lovell.
Jan. 1, 1844	Hundley, Granville, and Louisa Odle.
Jan. 26, 1849	Hundley, Hiram B., and Martha Edwards.
Dec. 13, 1841	Hundley, Josiah, and Emily Lyell.
Dec. 19, 1838	Hunley, William, and Nancy Lyell, dau. of Mary Ann Lyell.
May 25, 1780	Hunt, James, and Sarah Tarry.
Nov. 25, 1805	Hunt, John, and Nancy McCullough.
Jan. 9, 1809	Hunter, Alexander, and Sally M. Rowland.
July 27, 1801	Hunter, George, and Rachel Hibbs.
Jan. 12, 1824	Hunter, John, and Nancy Coleman, consent of John Coleman.
Aug. 8, 1804	Hunter, Peyton, and Raymoth Ramey.
June 4, 1804	Hunter, Samuel, and Salley Pace, dau. of John Pace.
Nov. 2, 1834	Hutchison, John C., and Lucy Meredith, dau. of Elijah Meredith.
Jan. 2, 1841	Irby, William, and Mary Seay.
Aug. 19, 1816	Ivil, John, and Elizabeth E. Wells.
Sept. 16, 1846	Ivy, Nelson, and Catharine T. Wells.
Oct. 10, 1815	Ivy, John W., and Susannah Wells.
Oct. 7, 1833	Jackson, James, and Julia Craig, consent of Adam and Mary Craig.
Apr. 14, 1846	Jackson, James H., consent of Sarah Jackson, and Laura Eckhols, consent of Susan Echols.
Jan. 25, 1796	Jamerson, William, and Lizey Brown.
Dec. 2, 1794	Jameson, Thomas, and Hesey Huston (of Franklin Co.), dau. of William Huston.

Feb. 12, 1844	Jarrett, Robert, and Teresse Teel.
Oct. 28, 1819	Jenkins, Joseph, and Patsy Griffin, consent of Nancy Griffen.
Nov. 13, 1837	Jennings, Swafford W., and Betsy G. Fariss (or Pharis), dau. of Daniel Pharis.
Dec. 23, 1846	Johnson, William, and Luticia Pearson.
Nov. 10, 1835	Joice, Alexander, and Mary E. Taylor, dau. of Reubin Taylor.
Jan. 21, 1802	Jones, Ambrose, and Polley Lesueur, dau. of Martel Lesueur.
Dec. 21, 1825	Jones, Armistead, and Cassandra Barrow, dau. of William Barrow.
Jan. 2, 1817	Jones, Austin, and Ruth Shelton.
May 25, 1831	Jones, Bird, and Nancy Roach.
Mar. 23, 1818	Jones, Buckner, and Hannah Martin.
Oct. 11, 1795	Jones, Charles, and Polley King, dau. of John King, consent only.
Dec. 14, 1835	Jones, Daniel, consent of Wilson Jones, and Cynthia Harris, dau. of Cynthia Harris.
Dec. 10, 1827	Jones, George, and Ann King.
Dec. 18, 1830	Jones, Greenwood, and Rachel Dyer, dau. of Mary Dyer.
Jan. 20, 1823	Jones, John L., consent of A. Jones, and Nelly Barber, dau. of Fanny Barber.
Mar. 6, 1838	Jones, Joseph M., and Margaret C. Davis, dau. of Peter Davis.
Nov. 5, 1804	Jones, Peter, and Elizabeth Reynolds.
June 20, 1785	Jones, Robert, and Susa (?) Richards.
July 2, 1802	Jones, Thomas, and Elizabeth Dalton Lyell, dau. of Joseph Lyell.
Nov. 23, 1809	Jones, Willis, and Betsy Hunt, consent only.
Sept. 27, 1816	Jones, Willis, and Lucy Hunt, dau. of Rody Hunt.
Dec. 17, 1823	Jones, Willis, and Mary George.
June 25, 1792	Joyce, Andrew, and Betsey King.
Dec. 7, 1841	Joyce, Thomas, and Martha M. Hill, consent of

Dec. 18, 1793   Kannon, James, and Patsey Willson.

Jan. 24, 1814   Keenum, George, and Elizabeth Stone.

Mar. 29, 1830   Kellam, Horatio, and Abigail, Burrus, dau. of
John Burrus.

Dec. 24, 1806   Kelley, Mason, and Sarah Chowning, dau. of
Hannah Chowning.

Sept. 11, 1801   Kelley, Thomas, and Letty Grogan, consent of John
Grogan.

Oct. 27, 1846   Kellum, William, and Eliza Marshall, consent of
James D. Marshall.

Feb. 10, 1781   Kelly, John, and Bettey Bybee, consent only.

Dec. 29, 1800   Kelly, John, and Rachel Davis.

Sept. 8, 1835   Kennerly, John W., and Elizabeth Cheatham, dau. of
Jane Athey.

Dec. 22, 1800   Key, Dabney, and Elizabeth Larason, dau. of
Peter Larason.

Dec. 18, 1814   Kimbrough, William, and Susannah Wiatt, dau. of
Vincent Wiatt.

May 6, 1816   King, George, and Susanna Martin.

Nov. 12, 1827   King, George, and Polley Waller, dau. of Jno. Waller.

Oct. 13, 1829   King, George, and Mary Cahill, dau. of Diannah Cahill.

Sept. 1, 1829   King, James, and Delila Wilson.

Mar. 17, 1822   King, John, and Eliza. Waller, consent of John Waller.

Oct. 18, 1841   King, Lewis G., and Elizabeth King, dau. of John King.

July 19, 1794   King, William, and Nancy Mitchell, dau. of
William Mitchell.

Nov. 11, 1816   Kington, Joseph, and Alice Suttenfield.

July 12, 1826   Kington, Reubin, and Sarah Burchett.

Jan. 12, 1780   Knox, Benjamin, and Jamima Gardner, dau. of
Wm. Gardner.

Dec. 7, 1827   Koger, John, and Gilley C. Napier, dau. of
Tarlton Napier.

Feb. 11, 1822   Kyle, James, and Elizabeth Jones.

Dec. 14, 1836   Lacy, Charles, H., and Susan C. Edwards, dau. of John Edwards.

July 1, 1833   Lamkin, Richard G., and Ann P. Bouldin.

Nov. 21, 1803   Lampkin, Lewis, and Angellico Ryan, dau. of Phillip Ryan.

Dec. 13, 1813   Land, Jachariah, and Milly Cox.

Mar. 9, 1846   Land, Meshack, and Rachael Robertson.

Jan. 29, 1844   Land, Nelson, and Dilly McDonald.

June 19, 1813   Land, Shadrick, and Ruth Wilson, "21 years of age."

Oct. 10, 1825   Land, William, and Liddy Wilson.

Dec. 17, 1807   Lanier, David, and Mary Reamey.

Nov. -- 1784   Lanier, Washington, and Elizabeth Hicks.

Dec. 28, 1807   Lansford, William, and Susanna Adams.

Oct. 26, 1807   Lark, Robert, and Elizabeth Norriss.

Sept. 10, 1821   Larrison, Peter, and Janett Cox.

Feb. 23, 1807   Larrison, James, and Nancy Norman.

Oct. 25, 1845   Law, David F. and Averilla Law, dau. of Adam Law.

Nov. 28, 1846   Law, James B., and Rayney Lawrence, dau. of Henry Lawrence.

Dec. 29, 1830   Lawrence, Arthur F., and Polly Pearson, dau. of John Pearson.

Jan. 9, 1832   Lawrence, James H., and Elizabeth Pearson.

Feb. 5, 1820   Lawrence, Henry, and Gilley Allen.

Sept. 14, 1801   Lawrence, James, and Martha Johnston.

Nov. -- 1846   Lawrence, James H., and Ann Smith, dau. of Nancy Smith.

Mar. 9, 1836   Leak, Dabney F., and Agnes Doyle.

May 24, 1843   Leake, Andrew J., and Jane Hereford.

Oct. 13, 1817   Leake, Garland, and Polly Rea.

Feb. 13, 1826	Leake, Garland, and Harriett Doyle.
Feb. 24, 1822	Leake, Robert, and Sally Lawless.
May 27, 1821	Leffel, Thomas, and Sidney Birchett.
Apr. 9, 1821	Lemon (?), Jefferson, and Rena Barker (?).
Nov. 4, 1828	Lemons, William, and Mary McDaniel, dau. of Zere (?) McDaniel.
Feb. 18, 1839	Lester, Daniel, and Nancy Hicks, dau. of Thomas C. Hicks.
Oct. 14, 1839	Lester, Jesse, and America Trent.
Jan. 12, 1829	Lester, Thomas, and Frances King, dau. of Joseph King.
Aug. 4, 1803	Letcher, James, and Healin Garner, dau. of Sarah Garner.
Oct. 25, 1792	Letchworth, Benjamin, and Eleanor Adams.
Nov. 9, 1840	Lewis, Deverous, and Arrenia Clifton, dau. of John Clifton.
Mar. 11, 1811	Lewis, John, and Sarah Davis.
Nov. 26, 1791	Lindsey, Henry, and Elizabeth Smith, dau. of Daniel Smith.
Feb. 5, 1829	Lindsey, James, and Nancy Smith.
July 30, 1821	Lindsey, John, and Polly G. Rea.
July 9, 1821	Lindsey, Joshua, and Dolly Anderson.
June 15, 1812	Litterell, Ire, and Polly Shoemate.
Feb. 14, 1807	Long, Gabriel, and Sally Humphrys.
Aug. 14, 1823	Lovell, Daniel, and Nancy Wyatt.
June 3, 1785	Lovell, Markham, and -----Jones, dau. of Ambrose Jones.
Dec. 17, 1812	Lovell, William, and Polly Odaniel.
Oct. 4, 1830	Loyd, Thomas, and Nancy Higgs.
Mar. 1, 1805	Lyell, Richard, and Agatha Dickerson, dau. of Thos. Dickerson.
Aug. 12, 1816	Lyell, Richard, and Ava Hensley.

Mar. 1, 1805	Lyell, Robert, and Deborah Lawrence, dau. of Henry Lawrence.
Nov. 28, 1836	Lyle, Jefferson, and Parthenia G. Stultz.
Jan. 4, 1821	Mabe, Reubin, and Nancy Gilley.
Feb. 23, 1812	Mabe, William, and Eliza. Taylor.
Oct. 22, 1818	Mageehee, Angus, and Patsey Thornton, dau. of Henry Thornton.
Feb. 12, 1818	Maghee, Martin, and Sarah Heard, dau. of Nancy Heard.
Jan. 29, 1828	Mahon, Edmund, and Polly Casey, consent of Martha Casey.
Dec. 13, 1845	Mahon, Reuben, and Virginia E. Harris, grdn. Orson Martin.
Oct. 25, 1828	Mahon, William, and Salley Bryant, dau. of Eliza. Bryant.
Jan. 24, 1821	Mahon, Willis, and Mary Gilley, dau. of Francis Gilley.
Dec. 19, 1817	Major, James, and Nancy Abingdon, dau. of Henry Abington.
Feb. 18, 1846	Mann, Benja., and Aggy Cousins.
Sept. 5, 1849	Mann, George, and Emeline Beck.
Oct. 13, 1828	Mann, William (or Buck), and Betsey Stewart.
Oct. 22, 1849	Manning, Samuel, and Elizabeth Moon, dau. of James R. Going by adoption.
Aug. 14, 1821	Marshall, Benjamin, and Nancy Nance, dau. of Nancy Nance.
Apr. 30, 1819	Marshall, Elias, and Frances West, dau. of Nicholas West, consent only.
May 22, 1820	Marshall, James D., and Susannah Weaver.
June 30, 1849	Marshall, John W., and Eliza Ann Dunavant, dau. of Thomas Dunavant.
May 15, 1835	Marshall, Madison, and Virginia Lane, dau. of Rebecca Lane.
June 16, 1849	Marshall, Reuben D., and Harriet E. Cole, dau. of Thos. Cole.
Dec. 24, 1840	Marshall, Whittington, and Catharine McDaniel, dau. of Zere McDaniel.

Oct. 10, 1802 Marshall, William, and Eveland Warren.

Oct. 27, 1846 Marshall, William, and Tabitha C. Epperson, consent of Anthony Epperson.

Nov. 23, 1824 Martin, Abner, and Jane Jones, consent of Thomas Jones.

Jan. 31, 1827 Martin, Abraham, and Nancy Gunnell, dau. of James G. Gunnell, Sr.

Aug. 12, 1833 Martin, Bailey, and Mary Dyer.

May 9, 1846 Martin, Charles F., and Sarah Lawrence, dau. of Henry Lawrence.

Sept. 8, 1823 Martin, Early, and Doratha Pyrtle.

Feb. 22, 1808 Martin, George, and Charlotte Davis.

Dec. 17, 1830 Martin, George W., and Elizabeth A. Starling.

Sept. 8, 1819 Martin, Hudson, and Mary Taylor.

June 4, 1827 Martin, Isaac, and Elizabeth Smith.

May 7, 1838 Martin, Jesse G., and Matilda Bryant.

--- --- 1810 Martin, Joel, and Hannah Roberts.

Jan. 28, 1805 Martin, Joshua, and Tibitha Mullins.

Oct. 20, 1826 Martin, Orson, and Mary Jones, consent of Thomas Jones.

Apr. 8, 1833 Martin, Richard, and Lucy A. Taylor, dau. of R. Taylor.

Oct. 31, 1801 Martin, William, and Polly Fearney.

Dec. 6, 1836 Martin, William, and Susan Hairston, dau. of George Hairston.

Nov. 8, 1842 Martin, William O., and Mary K. Riddle, dau. of Lucy B. Riddle.

Dec. 14, 1818 Mason, Carter W., and Elizabeth Moore.

Aug. 12, 1816 Mason, David, and Sarah Mabe.

May 27, 1832 Massey, James Adison, and Jane Martin, "aged 22 last month."

July 12, 1792 Mastin, Jacob, and Eliza. Melvin, consent only.

Oct. 26, 1801 Mastin, John, and Anna Holmes.

Feb. 27, 1837	Mathews, Calvin, and Lucy Mullins, dau. of Henry G. Mullins.
Dec. 12, 1842	Mathews, Claiborne, and Jane Eggleton.
Nov. 18, 1841	Mathews, Coleman, and Mildred Eggleton, dau. of Thomas Eggleton.
Nov. 20, 1823	Mathews, James, and Eliza. D. Allen.
Dec. 11, 1840	Mathews, Tandey, and Susan Mullins.
June 30, 1794	Mathews, William, and Elizabeth Hunter.
Aug. 28, 1827	Mathews, William, and Mary S. Staples, dau. of George S. Staples.
June 17, 1835	Matthews, Dabney W., and Lucy Matthews.
Feb. 10, 1817	Mattock, William, and Ruth Atkisson, dau. of Ruth Atkisson.
Sept. 18, 1802	Maupin, George, and Jeane Warren, dau. of William Warren.
Sept. 2, 1808	Maupin, Jessee, and Susannah Dent.
May 7, 1809	Maupin, Morgan, and Martha Burchett.
July 31, 1804	Maupin, William, and Caty Hardy.
June 24, 1779	May, John, and Charity Taylor, dau. of James Taylor.
Oct. 21, 1841	May, Sanford, and Martha A. Whirly, dau. of Mary Wherly.
Oct. 15, 1799	Mayner, Jeremiah, and Nancy Miller.
Dec. 2, 1799	Mayner, Stephen, and Polley Cradock.
Dec. 25, 1811	Mays, Jessee, and Judith Wade, dau. of Ballenger Wade.
Jan. 6, 1829	McBride, Jacob, and Dessa Wills, dau. of Nelson Wills.
Sept. 13, 1816	McClane, Wm., and Caroline House.
Jan. 9, 1809	McCrow, Geo., and Penelope C. Waller.
Feb. 27, 1797	McCullock, Alexander, and Susanah Nance.
Mar. 18, 1805	McCullough, James, and Faney King.
Jan. 23, 1831	McDaniel, James, and Elizabeth Goodman, dau. of John Goodman.
Feb. 20, 1830	McDaniel, Joel, and Zerichia Taylor, dau. of John Taylor.

Apr. 3, 1836	McDaniel, John, and Phoeba Sampson.
Feb. 5, 1817	McKenny, Henry, and Hannah Burton, consent of David Burton.
Oct. 19, 1797	McKinney, Kinney, and Phebee Hensley.
Sept. 10, 1838	McMillion, John, and Eliza H. Pleaster.
Feb. 27, 1843	Meaks, Calvin W., and Nancy Dunn, dau. of Martha Dunn.
Aug. 8, 1831	Means, Thomas P., and Dicey Fee.
Oct. 30, 1797	Medley, John, and Ann Carter, consent of Jesse Carter.
Jan. 10, 1826	Meeks, Coleman, and Susannah Jones.
June 24, 1795	Melvin, James, and Caty Cannon.
Nov. 5, 1822	Menzies, John C., and Pamelia Jones.
July 11, 1797	Meredith, Elijah, and Frances Maupin, dau. of Jessee Maupin.
Aug. 12, 1816	Meredith, John, and Polly McBride.
Nov. 26, 1798	Meredith, Joseph, and Susana Murphy, dau. of James Murphy, Sr.
Dec. 31, 1803	Meredith, William, and Rosey Heard, dau. of Wm. Heard.
Dec. 23, 1820	Merrick, Edward, and Martha Smith, dau. of Sally Smith.
Dec. 14, 1846	Miles, Lawson H., and Eliza Montgomery.
Oct. 3, 1842	Millener, Marguis D. L., and Sarah Ann Tinsley, dau. of D. M. Tinsley.
July 31, 1828	Millner, Thomas B., and Sarah McDaniel, dau. of Jere (?) and Katharine McDaniel.
July 23, 1845	Millner, Thomas F., and Mary Ann Tinsley.
Sept. 9, 1803	Mills, Aaron, and Sally Shelton.
Nov. 3, 1807	Mills, Francis, and Salley Moore.
Feb. 31, 1849	Mills, James B., and Mariah G. Nunn.
Dec. 19, 1844	Mills, Richard, and Judith Poindexter, 21 years of age. Emily and Morris Mapier, affidavit as to age for wife.

Dec. 18, 1843   Mills, Robert Wiley, and Mary Jarrett, dau. of
Allen Jarrett.

Jan. 9, 1801   Mills, William F., and Susanna Allen.

Dec. 3, 1845   Mills, William, and Martha Mills, dau. of
James B. Mills.

Sept. 19, 1795   Miner, Heyekiah, and Elizabeth Going.

Jan. 1, 1842   Minter, Joseph, and Nancy Norman, grdn. Polly J.
Fretwell, "late Polly J. Norman."

Nov. 9, 1846   Minter, Joseph, and Margaret Davis.

Dec. 7, 1799   Minter, Otheniel, and Joyce Stults.

June 12, 1837   Minter, Othniel, and Mary Burgess.

Nov. 26, 1840   Minter, Richard W., and Mary Ann Doyle, dau. of
Samuel Doyle.

Nov. 19, 1813   Minter, Silas, and Nancy Stults, consent of Abner Stults.

Apr. 24, 1845   Minter, Silas, and Betsey Philpott.

Oct. 21, 1846   Minter, Silas, and Jane A. Eggleton, dau. of
Michael Eggleton.

Feb. 20, 1843   Minter, William L., and Mary D. Burgess, dau. of
Polly Minter. Othniel Minter, grdn. of wife.

Jan. 8, 1849   Minter, Williamson, and Julian Law.

Dec. 17, 1842   Mitchell, Archibald W., and Sarah O. Norman, grdn.
Polly J. Fretwell, "late Polly J. Norman."

Nov. 19, 1842   Mitchell, Granville, and Martha Ann Clark, dau. of
Casandra Clark.

Nov. 11, 1844   Mitchell, Ignatius F., and Lucy Jane Holt.

Mar. 9, 1846   Mitchell, Jesse T., and Roxy A. Thompson, dau.
of Robert H. Thompson.

Sept. 23, 1845   Mitchell, Joel L., and Balzora Bauldin, dau. of
Patsy C. Bauldin.

Dec. 5, 1846   Mitchell, Robert, and Ann Heard.

May 30, 1778   Mitchell, William, and Martha Stokes.

Nov. 24, 1814   Montgomery, John, and Elizabeth Jones, dau. of
Joseph Jones.

Apr. 30, 1832   Montgomery, John, and Delila Shumate, dau. of
Saml. Shumate.

Feb. 19, 1798	Moore, Alexander, and Elizabeth Pace.
Aug. 29, 1795	Moore, Charles, and Elizabeth Going.
May 13, 1778	Moore, Shallen (or Stratton), and Ann Hooker, dau. of Robt. Hooker.
Aug. 11, 1826	Moore, Thomas, and Frances Rea.
Feb. 25, 1805	Moore, William, and Eliza. Carter.
Dec. 11, 1837	Moore, Wm. B., and Nancy L. Mays.
Jan. 16, 1823	Moore, William, and Ellenor Gravley, dau. of Jabez Gravely.
Feb. 2, 1838	Moorman, Edwin W., and Sally S. Bird.
Nov. 12, 1806	Morris, William, and Tabitha Cheatham.
Mar. 10, 1841	Morris, William B., grdn. Wm. J. Hamlett, and Caroline Philpott, grdn. John L. Wootton.
Jan. 9, 1837	Morris, Woodson, and Mary D. Philpott.
Feb. 9, 1805	Morriss, Archibald, and Martha Cheatham.
Apr. 14, 1815	Mullin, David, and Polly Burgess.
Nov. 18, 1815	Mullins, Henry G., and Matilda W. Hill.
Jan. 29, 1798	Mullins, Thomas, and Amy Gilpin, dau. of Sarah Gilpin.
Sept. 15, 1818	Murfry, James, and Elizabeth Hind.
Nov. 7, 1794	Murphy, Gabriel, and Ruth Peregoy, consent of Robert Peregoy, consent only.
June 30, 1812	Murphy, James, and Eliza. Norriss.
Oct. 30, 1816	Murphy, Peyton, and Mary Graveley, consent of Joseph Graveley.
Dec. 10, 1799	Nance, Allen, and Bettsey Nance, dau. of John Nance.
Aug. 27, 1846	Nance, Fontaine, and Jemima Vincent Grant, dau. of Archibald Grant.
Dec. 28, 1849	Nance, James, and Nancy Dalton.
Dec. 13, 1813	Nance, Peyton, and Polly W. King, dau. of John King, "son of George."
Nov. 15, 1836	Nance, Pleasant, and Eliza Barker, dau. of Allen Barker.
June 6, 1814	Nance, Stephen, and Sarah M. Hughes, dau. of A. Hughes.

July 12, 1822   Nance, Terrell, and Eliza. Oakes, consent of
Hannah Oakes.

Feb. 13, 1821   Neblett, William S. (of Franklin County), and Mary Ann
Chily (or Cheeley), dau. of Cuthbert Cheely.

Mar. 8, 1832   Nicholas, Greenberry, and America Spencer.

Dec. 4, 1793   Nicholls, David, and Clarry Rowland.

Mar. 20, 1802   Nichols, Thomas, and Salley Lane.

May 30, 1792   Noe, Gideon (of Patrick County), and Lucy Price.

Feb. 20, 1843   Norman, Courtney W., and Elizabeth J. Mitchell,
consent of Coleman and Elizabeth Mitchell.

Sept. 27, 1812   Norman, Dutton, and Caty Larrison.

Nov. 14, 1842   Norman, James B., and Lucy W. Price.

Nov. 29, 1819   Norman, Nelson, and Polly Oaks.

Dec. 14, 1793   Norris, Ezebulon, and Elizabeth Dillingham.

Dec. 1, 1810   Norriss, Samuel, and Betsey Pedigo.

May 26, 1794   Northcutt, Francis, and Lucy Haley.

July 26, 1783   Norton, John, and Sarah Penn, dau. of Philip Penn.

Aug. 7, 1801   Nucum, Cary, and Margaret Akin, consent of
Nicholas and Jean Akin.

Aug. 4, 1841   Nunn, George W., and Mariah G. Minter, dau. of
Othniel Minter.

Apr. 29, 1823   Nunn, Joel P., and Sally V. Clark.

Oct. 9, 1810   Nunn, Joseph, and ----- -----

Oct. 1, 1849   Nunn, Josiah W., and Lavina A. Pedigo, dau. of
Joseph and Sara Pedigo.

Oct. 8, 1845   Nunn, Riley, and Jane Thomasson.

Oct. 8, 1838   Nunn, Stephen, and Louisa Edwards.

Jan. 14, 1794   Nunn, Thomas, and Jean Pace.

Oct. 31, 1809   Nunn, Thomas, and Franky Clarke.

Mar. 24, 1800   Nunn, Waters, and Salley Wash.

Mar. 28, 1805   Nunn, William, and Elizabeth Clark.

May 15, 1835	Nunnally, Thos. W., and Eliza J. Willson.
Jan. 14, 1811	Oakley, William, and Milley Quarles.
Aug. 29, 1836	Oakley, William M., and Icypeana Mills, dau. of Aaron Mills.
Dec. 14, 1840	Odell, Joseph, and Elizabeth Anderson.
Jan. 1, 1842	Odle, James, and Sereney Gilley.
June 13, 1821	Odle, John, and Nancy Bailey.
Jan. 13, 1845	Odle, William W., consent of George Odle, and Caroline M. Gilley, consent of Peter and Arria Gilley.
Oct. 30, 1797	Officer, Thomas, and Susannah Dillion.
Dec. 27, 1813	Oldham, William, and Peggy Clarke, dau. of James and Sally Clarke.
Jan. 17, 1783	O'Neal, Basil, and Milley Briscoe, dau. of John Briscoe.
Jan. 26, 1846	Oxley, Alfred, and Sally Goode, dau. of Samuel Goode.
Mar. -- 1825	Pace, Daniel, and Jane King.
Mar. 10, 1828	Pace, Francis, and Sarah Deshazo, dau. of William Deshazo.
Sept. -- 1828	Pace, James B., grdn, Jeremiah Baker, and Caroline M. Hunter.
Oct. 5, 1841	Pace,Jerman W., and Harriet M. Williams.
Dec. 24, 1803	Pace, John, and Hanah Hefflefinger, dau. of John Hefflefinger.
Dec. 8, 1817	Pace, Thomas, and Bethenia Hardy.
Feb. 21, 1820	Palmer, Elijah, and Coatney Cassady.
Oct. 29, 1798	Pannell, David, and Parthenia Letcher.
May 10, 1784	Parberry, James, and Ann Graves, dau. of William Graves.
Mar. 25, 1799	Parks, Joseph, and Caty Kelley.
Jan. 10, 1814	Parish, Allen, and Frances Hunt.
Sept. 12, 1831	Parish, Lee, and Polly Pulliam.

Sept. 19, 1802	Parsley, James, and Armin Warren, dau. of William Warren.
Sept. 28, 1801	Parsley, William, and Sarah Maupin, dau. of Lucy Maupin.
Sept. 26, 1804	Parsley, William, and Amey Pedigo.
Oct. 13, 1794	Patrick, James, and Sarah Dunlap.
Nov. 22, 1830	Patterson, Jarrott, and Lucy Payne, consent of Daniel Payne.
Nov. 26, 1804	Paul, John, and Sarah Akin, dau. of Nicholas and Jane Akin.
July -- 1826	Payne, John L., and Fanny Thomasson, dau. of Arnold Thomasson.
Mar. 14, 1811	Payne, Robert, and Nancy Carter.
May 18, 1812	Payne, Robert, and Jane Hereford.
Dec. 9, 1844	Payne, Ryland, and Margaret E. Cox.
Jan. 13, 1816	Payne, Thomas, and Amy G. Bouldin.
Feb. 24, 1830	Payne, William, and Letty Ann Bouldin, consent of Thos. Bouldin.
Dec. 28, 1807	Payne, Wryland, and Polly Carter.
Oct. 12, 1835	Pearson, James, and Rebecca Matthews.
May 6, 1794	Pearson, Meredith, and Rhoda Delozer.
Dec. 23, 1830	Pearson, Peyton, and Polly Smith.
Feb. 14, 1824	Pease, Edward, and Martha Fifer.
Aug. 26, 1779	Peck, David, and Jean Martin, dau. of Jas. Martin.
Feb. 20, 1820	Peddigo, Henry, and Malinda Poston.
Sept. 9, 1824	Peddigo, John, and Charity Posten.
Jan. 13, 1812	Peddigo, Moses, and Polly Agee.
Jan. 3, 1792	Peddigo, Robert, and ----- -----
Jan. 8, 1816	Pedigo, Elijah, and Sarah Poston.
Feb. 1, 1845	Pedigo, Henry S., and Mary Ann Smith.
Oct. 13, 1845	Pedigo, John L., and Elizabeth Shewmate.
Oct. 18, 1800	Pelfrey, James, and Polly Turner.
Apr. 19, 1823	Pemberton, Richard, and Sarah Bondurant, dau. of Claiborn Bondurant.

Aug. 11, 1829   Penn, Columbus, and Francis Rives.

Dec. 8, 1784   Penn, George, and Patty Farriss, dau. of Jacob Farriss.

Nov. 10, 1818   Penn, James, and Mary Shelton.

Apr. 15, 1834   Penn, Peter P., and Elizabeth McDonald.

Aug. 22, 1803   Pennell, John, and Milley Hunter, consent of Titus Hunter.

Oct. 20, 1842   Perkins, James H., and Amanda Trotter.

Aug. 29, 1829   Perkins, Jesse, and Mary Fontaine.

Jan. 4, 1817   Perkins, Joseph, and Elizabeth Clanton, dau. of
George Clanton.

Dec. 25, 1811   Perkins, William, and Rebecca Miller.

Mar. 13, 1830   Perkins, William, Sr., and Martha H. Fontaine.

Oct. 10, 1825   Perkinson, Hezekiah, and Susannah Philpott.

Jan. 10, 1825   Perkinson, William, and Ferbe Lawrence.

Oct. 20, 1846   Peters, Dr. Henry D., and Mary F. Gravely, dau.
of George Gravely.

Aug. 5, 1823   Pettit, John, and Mary Dillion.

Feb. 25, 1836   Petty, Davis M., and Sarah Childress.

July 25, 1849   Petty, Isham M., and Mary Evins.

Dec. 11, 1839   Phariss, George W., and Pamelia Holt, dau. of
Elizabeth Holt.

Jan. 5, 1814   Phifer, Forrest, and Susannah Philpott, consent of
Samuel Philpott.

May 10, 1813   Phifer, James, and Jane Turner, dau. of William Turner.

July 22, 1817   Phifer, John, and Elizabeth Jones Philpott, consent of
Samuel Philpott.

July 25, 1808   Phifer, Joseph, and Lindy Witt.

June 9, 1823   Phillips, Alexander, and Sarah Dillen, dau. of
Charlotte Dillen.

Dec. 29, 1806   Phillips, Elisha, and Susanna Rea.

Mar. 17, 1810   Phillips, Lewis, and ----- -----

Jan. 2, 1806   Philpott, Allen, and Mary Ann Philpott.

Sept. 30, 1823   Philpott, Charles, and Mary D. Bassett.

Jan. 30, 1811   Philpott, David, and Sarah Nance.

Aug. 14, 1826   Philpott, David, and Diannah Cahill, dau. of Diannah Cahill.

Apr. 10, 1837   Philpott, Garrett, and Elizabeth Clanton.

Jan. 14, 1811   Philpott , John W. , and Elizabeth Dillen.

Dec. -- 1815   Philpott, John, and Sidney Munroe.

Jan. 6, 1819   Philpott, John, and Nancy Phyfer, consent of Joseph Phifer.

Oct. 12, 1835   Philpott, John J. , and Elizabeth R. Walker, dau. of
                  Arnold Walker.

Oct. 3, 1836   Philpott, Samuel, and Margaret Pyrtle, dau. of Mary Pyrtle.

Nov. 11, 1811   Philpott, Zachariah, and Nancy Cahill, consent of
                  John Cahill.

June 23, 1828   Pierce, Harrison, and Nancy Scales.

July 2, 1781   Pitman, James, and Martha Taylor.

July 20, 1811   Pleasted (?), Joshua, and Nancy Jarviss.

--- -- 183-?   Poindexter, John, and Louisa Mills.

Nov. 30, 1801   Poston, Edward, and Pheby Parsley.

Oct. 14, 1818   Poston, Solomon, and Bethenia Roberts.

Aug. 27, 1825   Potter, Gidean R. , and Jemimah Rea, dau. of James Rea.

Dec. 16, 1830   Pratt, Felix, and Patience Wells.

Aug. 25, 1838   Pratt, George, and Ruth Snell.

Nov. 14, 1825   Pratt, John, and Trifinia Stratton.

Sept. 4, 1831   Pratt, William J. , and Mary Robertson.

Jan. 6, 1840   Prewit, Elijah, and Ann Clanton.

Apr. 3, 1845   Price, Allen, and Biddy Moore, dau. of James Moore.

Dec. 12, 1826   Price, Duke, and Rachel W. Trent.

Dec. 11, 1837   Price, Duke, and Harriet M. Shackleford, dau. of
                  Wm. Shackleford, Sr.

Feb. 8, 1836   Price, Isaac B. , and Louisa Lanier, dau. of
                  Benjamin Lanier.

May 9, 1825	Price, John, and Lucy Pratt, dau. of John Pratt.
Dec. 30, 1844	Price, James, and Mary E. Cahill.
July 13, 1842	Price, John, and Lucy W. Harris.
Dec. 29, 1845	Price, Rece, and Lucinda Moore, dau. of James Moore.
Jan. 20, 1836	Price, Williamson E., and Frances Baker.
June 4, 1845	Price, Zaid W., and Eliza Lemmons, dau. of Jefferson Lemmons.
Oct. 14, 1822	Pritchett, Henry, and Martha M. Waller, dau. of Carr Waller.
Sept. 17, 1839	Pritchett, Richard H., and Lucinda S. Hill.
Feb. 23, 1807	Proctor, Lewis, and Joyce Haley, dau. of James Hailey.
Jan. 31, 1843	Pruitt, John, and Dolley Clanton.
Sept. 14, 1818	Pulliam, Drury, and Mary Shackelford, dau. of William Shackleford.
May 27, 1844	Pulliam, Drury, and Parthenia Clanton, dau. of Winnifred Clanton.
Feb. 11, 1842	Pulliam, William, and Franky Cox, dau. of William Cox.
Dec. 9, 1832	Pullin, Thomas, and Sarah Cheeley, dau. of Cuthbert Cheeley.
Nov. 23, 1830	Purdy, Anderson, and Lucy Maupin, dau. of William Maupin.
Mar. 1, 1815	Pyrtle, Barton, and Lucinda Martin, dau. of Sary Martin.
Oct. -- 1815	Pyrtle, Carr, and Margaret Hurd.
Nov. 23, 1791	Quarles, James, and Elizabeth Pelphry, dau. of John Pelphry.
Jan. 12, 1846	Quimby, William, and Kesiah Pankey.
June 4, 1826	Ragin, John, and Matilda Odle.
Dec. 18, 1805	Ragsdill, Thomas, and Lucy Lanier, dau. of David Lanier.

Nov. 19, 1849	Ramsey, Lacy, and Elizabeth Nunn.
Sept. 8, 1838	Ramsey, Woodson, and Mary C. Davis.
Nov. 30, 1793	Ray, Joseph, and Mary Ann Hayse, consent of William Hays.
Jan. 2, 1814	Ray, Reuben, and Eliza. Rogers.
July 19, 1806	Raynolds, John, and Sarah Phillpott, dau. of Charles Thomas Phillpott.
Dec. 26, 1796	Rea, Abner, and Nancy Rea, dau. of John Phillips.
Feb. 17, 1826	Rea (or Wray), Bruce, and Polly Cox.
Jan. 26, 1830	Rea, Edmund J., and Pemelia J. Clinkscales, dau. of Wm. Clinkscales.
Feb. 29, 1808	Rea, George, and Prudence Rea.
Nov. 30, 1807	Rea, James, and Polley, Reamy, consent of Louis Reamy.
Sept. 24, 1814	Rea, James, and Judia Francis.
Jan. 27, 1827	Rea, James, and Elizabeth Hewlett.
July 28, 1806	Rea, John, and Jeaney Woodleif.
Dec. 20, 1831	Rea, John B., and Biddy Moore, consent of Elexander Moore.
Nov. 11, 1816	Rea, Joseph, and Mary West, dau. of Nicholas West.
Sept. 13, 1841	Rea, Iredell J., and Virginia Salmon, dau. of John Salmon.
Jan. 11, 1796	Rea, Wilson, son of William C. Rea, and Fanny Franklin.
Dec. 2, 1814	Reamey, James, and Leticia Hughes.
July 21, 1849	Reamy, Peter R., son of D. Reamy, and Sarah J. Waller, dau. of George Waller.
Sept. 11, 1831	Redd, Edmund B., and Sarah Ann Fontaine.
Sept. 2, 1813	Redd, Overton, and Martha Fontaine, dau. of P. H. Fontaine.
Apr. 22, 1779	Rentfro, Mark, and Noami Standifore.
June 12, 1779	Reynolds, George, and Susanna Lansford, dau. of Catherine Lansford (of Pittsylvania Co.).

Apr. 16, 1821	Reynolds, William, and Lucy Burchett.
Nov. 18, 1844	Rice, John D., and Eliza Ann Gravely.
Oct. 28, 1779	Richards, Shadrick, and Susannah Hamilton, dau. of ----- Hamilton, widow.
Dec. 19, 1838	Richardson, Abner, and Nancy Minter, dau. of Silas Minter.
Aug. 6, 1839	Richardson, Arthur, and Mary J. Fleemon, dau. of George Fleemon.
Nov. 19, 1834	Richardson, George, and Clarissa Martin, dau. of Jesse Martin.
Dec. 27, 1817	Richardson, James, and Catharine Haley, dau. of Thomas Haley.
Jan. 16, 1779	Richardson, John, and Mary Ryan, dau. of William Ryan.
May 7, 1811	Richardson, John, and Elizabeth Stults, consent of Abner Stults.
Dec. 7, 1839	Richardson, John, and Susan Lester, dau. of John Lester.
Feb. 12, 1849	Rickman, William H., and Sarah Hundly.
Dec. 8, 1826	Riddle, Ephriam, and Judith Gravely.
June 9, 1821	Riddle, Thomas, and Lucy Johnston.
Apr. 11, 1831	Rily, Daniel, and Lucinda Rea, dau. of Joseph Rea.
Jan. 27, 1840	Roach, James, and Matilda Cayton, dau. of Cornelius Cayton.
Dec. 12, 1825	Roberts, James, and Ann Meredith.
Mar. 26, 1804	Roberts, John, and Mary Akin, dau. of Nicholas and Jane Akin.
Aug. 28, 1809	Roberts, Lewis, and Polly Joy.
Sept. 25, 1816	Robertson, James, and Betsey Smith.
Oct. 24, 1839	Robertson, John C., and Mary Lewis, dau. of John Lewis.
Nov. 15, 1827	Robertson, Joseph, and Rachel Rea.
Oct. 26, 1836	Robertson, Joseph, and Permelia Wilson.
June 28, 1824	Rogers, William, and Susannah Perdie.

May 8, 1782	Rowland, Baldwin, and Sarah Hairston, dau. of Robert Hairston.
June 17, 1820	Rowland, Creed, and Matilda Brewer, dau. of Nancy Brewer.
Mar. 24, 1811	Rowland, Gilbert, brother of Washington Rowland, and Polly Bouldin (?).
July 23, 1780	Rowland, John, and Enes Sturgeon.
Jan. 4, 1803	Rowland, John, Jr., and Elizabeth Wash, dau, of John Wash.
June 20, 1778	Rowland, Michael, and Elizabeth Hairston.
Aug. 26, 1815	Rowland, Washington, and Nancy Bouldin.
Sept. 28, 1801	Rowland, William, and Milly Radford, dau. of Febe Radford.
Dec. 15, 1838	Royster, Banister, and Martha Terrell.
Jan. 7, 1811	Salmon, Hezekiah, and Hannah Gates.
Dec. 14, 1825	Salmon, James D., and Elizabeth Maupin, dau. of Wm. Maupin.
July 27, 1804	Salmon, John, and Abigail Salmon.
Apr. 23, 1805	Salmon, Noah, and Jeaney Henslee.
Mar. 26, 1794	Salmon, Thadeus, and Elizabeth Holmes.
June 26, 1843	Samms, Elijah, and Sally Nance, dau. of Hardin Nance.
Jan. 8, 1842	Samms, Elijah, and Caroline Watkins.
Jan. 12, 1821	Sams, John, and Nancy Pratt, dau. of John Pratt.
May 16, 1823	Sanders, William, and Ann W. Staples.
Jan. 2, 1809	Sandifer, Abraham, and Polly Phillips.
Feb. 20, 1778	Sanford (or Sandford), John, and Judith Garner.
Sept. 8, 1827	Scales, John, and Lucy Brewer.
May 12, 1828	Scales, John P., and Judith Shelton, dau. of Mary Shelton.
Sept. 19, 1834	Scales, Peter, and Lucinda Leake, grdn. Greenville Penn.
Sept. 12, 1836	Seawell, John T., and Elizabeth Hairston.

Oct. 29, 1798 Shackleford, Daniel, and Tabitha Nance, dau. of Reuben Nance.

Jan. 6, 1846 Shackleford, Wm., and Sophia W. Mathews.

Jan. 26, 1829 Shelton, Alfred, and Susannah Shelton.

Oct. 1, 1839 Shelton, James, and Adeline Jane Taylor, dau. of Reubin Taylor.

Aug. 25, 1838 Shelton, Joseph A., and Narcissa Morris, dau. of Jesse Aistrop.

July 29, 1799 Shelton, Leroy, and Nancy Lanier.

Apr. 13, 1802 Shelton, Nathan, and Polley Hatcher.

Mar. 19, 1832 Shelton, Peter, and Magdalene D. Watkins, dau. of Jno. Watkins.

Feb. 2, 1819 Shelton, Thomas S., and Elizabeth O. Norman, dau. of William Norman.

Mar. 25, 1799 Shields, James, and Mary McCullock.

Aug. 11, 1817 Shoemake, James, and Nancy Clark.

Mar. 11, 1805 Shoemate, Tollaver, and Lydia Clark.

Dec. 13, 1841 Shumate, Daniel, and Elizabeth Pace.

Feb. 9, 1846 Shumate, Samuel, and Nancy Pace.

Oct. 3, 1836 Shumate, Westley, and Josephine Pyrtle, dau. of Mary Pyrtle.

Sept. 19, 1827 Sigmon, William B., and Jane Moore, dau. of Benjamin Moore.

May 17, 1785 Simmons, Charles, and Elenor Cummins.

Dec. 12, 1826 Simms, John D., consent of James Simms, and Lucy Baker.

Aug. 31, 1801 Simpson, Presley, and Pattsey Southerland.

Jan. 7, 1799 Simpson, Rodham, and Polley Thomason.

Jan. 16, 1812 Simpson, Sanford, and Hopey Poston.

Nov. 23, 1844 Singleton, William, and America Ann Meade, consent of Morrison Meade.

Nov. 8, 1822 Slate, Isham, and Polley Chandler.

Sept. 24, 1831 Smith, Abner, and Elizabeth M. Hill.

Mar. 28, 1808 Smith, Allen, and Polly Brashears.

Dec. 19, 1808 Smith, Benjm., and Sally Hensley.

Nov. 24, 1835 Smith, Brice, and Jane Thommasson.

Nov. 11, 1816 Smith, Charles, and Sidny Pyrtle.

Feb. 13, 1822 Smith, Dabney, and Mary Melvin (?).

May 20, 1799 Smith, Daniel, and Polley Kennon.

Mar. 1, 1837 Smith, Daniel D., and Lucy B. Minter, dau. of Othniel Minter.

Mar. 17, 1845 Smith, David, and Sarah Dunavant, consent of Thomas Dunavant.

Apr. 27, 178-? Smith, Gideon, and Mary Hirston.

Nov. 5, 1804 Smith, James, and Sarah Hanna Phillpot.

Nov. 9, 1812 Smith, James, and Sally Grogan.

Mar. 13, 1828 Smith, James, M., and Martha W. Clark.

Sept. 15, 1824 Smith, John, and Betsy H. Jamerson. David Mays, consent for husband and wife.

May 18, 1823 Smith, Joseph, and Nancy Dillen, consent of Charlotte Dillen.

Feb. 27, 1809 Smith, Spenser, and Sally Creasey.

May 13, 1795 Smith, Thomas, and Betsey Alexander, dau. of John Alexander.

Mar. 29, 1798 Smith, Thomas, and Milly Cunningham.

June 30, 1800 Smith, William, and Polley Wade.

Dec. 23, 1816 Smith, William, and Patsy Creasy.

Dec. 24, 1833 Smith, William, and Elizabeth McMillion.

Nov. 18, 1813 Smoot, George W., and Agge Shoemate.

Dec. 30, 1816 Smoote, John B., and Delilah Shumate.

Mar. 19, 1796 Sneed, Alexander, and Elizabeth Jones.

Feb. 14, 1782 Snidow, Philip, and Baberry Prilliman.

Feb. 6, 1797 Soloman, Henry, and Mary Rea.

Sept. 5, 1836 Southall, William P., and Elizabeth P. Watkins, dau. of Jno.Watkins.

Aug. 24, 1843	Spencer, David H., and Mary Waller Dillard, dau. of Peter H. Dillard.
Aug. 23, 1803	Spencer, George, and Patty Hunter, dau. of Alexr. Hunter.
Mar. 19, 1835	Spencer, Nathaniel, and Martha Dyer, consent of D. Dyer.
Aug. 29, 1796	Spencer, John, and Ruth Dillard, dau. of John Dillard.
July 7, 1841	Spencer, John, and Nancy Dillion.
Apr. 29, 1804	Spencer, William, and Salley Hill.
Feb. 17, 1802	Sprouse, David, and Rachel Humphreys.
June 24, 1779	Standifore, Wm., and Jamima Jones, dau. of Thomas Jones.
June 15, 1785	Stanley, Joseph, and Sarah Kitchen.
Nov. 4, 1844	Stanley, Swinfield, and Lucinda Trent, dau. of Sarah Trent.
Jan. 7, 1804	Stanley, Thomas, and Hanna Birchett.
July 2, 1802	Staples, George, and Caroline Stovall.
Aug. 17, 1822	Staples, James, and Rhoda Virginia Nicolds, consent of Thomas Nicolds.
Oct. 12, 1813	Staples, Jno., and Sally Rentfroe.
May 30, 1824	Staples (or Stoops), John, and Elizabeth Cheely, dau. of Cuthbert Cheely.
June 9, 1826	Staples, John C., and Mary M. Martin, dau. of Jos. Martin.
Sept. 19, 1804	Staples, Norman, and Elizabeth Gordon.
Aug. 19, 1844	Starling, Edmund T., and Mary E. Anderson, grdn. Mary W. Morton.
May 22, 1803	Starling, Thomas, and Anna Redd, dau. of John Redd.
Jan. 7, 1831	Starling, William H., and Sarah T. Dandridge.
Jan. 26, 1839	Steagall, Alfred, and Ann King.
June 9, 1831	Stegall, Richard W., and Mary H. Morris.
Dec. 11, 1782	Stephen, Lyon, and Elley Perkins.

Feb. 6, 1832   Stephens, Coleman, and Jane Fee.

Nov. 4, 1823   Stephens, William A., and Salley Stacy, consent of Thomas Stacy.

June 17, 1792   Steward, William, and Milley Easter.

Jan. 31, 1803   Stewart, Alexander, and Nancy Delozer.

Dec. 11, 1817   Steward, David, and Ann Hancock.

Nov. 10, 1834   Stockton, Charles W., and Mary H. Barrow, dau. of William Barrow.

Nov. 7, 1837   Stockton, William L., and Susan E. Barrow, dau. of William and Susanna Barrow.

Sept. 13, 1835   Stokes, Allen, and Louisa Jones.

Dec. 1, 1837   Stokes, German, and Matilda Hunt, dau. of Rhody Hunt.

Sept. 11, 1820   Stone, Daniel, and Elizabeth M. Dilliard, dau. of George Dilliard.

July 25, 1846   Stone, James M., and Susan Elizabeth Martin, consent of Agner Martin.

July 10, 1792   Stone, John, and Mary Philpott, consent of Mary Ann and Jno. Philpott.

Feb. 22, 1842   Stone, Joseph P., and Lethia Ann Mitchell.

Feb. 9, 1818   Stone, Thos., and Mary Ann Stone.

Sept. 14, 1793   Stone, William, and Elizabeth Nunn.

June 14, 1819   Stone, Wm., and Patsy Philpott, consent of Samuel Philpott.

Jan. 5, 1837   Stovall, James R., and Lucinda T. Pace, consent of Mary Pace.

Dec. 14, 1818   Stratton, James, and Unity Gilley.

Aug. 23, 1837   Stratton, William Jackson, and Arminda Mahon, dau. of Willis Mahon.

Mar. 13, 1820   Stults, Adam, and Elizabeth Taylor.

Feb. 11, 1804   Stults, Gabriel, and Elizabeth Shackleford, dau. of William Shackleford.

Mar. 27, 1797   Stults, John, and Ann Melvin, dau. of Jas. Melvin.

Jan. 5, 1823   Stults, Joseph, and Lucy Egleton, dau. of Thomas Egleton.

Nov. 18, 1817	Stults, Thomas, and Susannah Minter.
Oct. 4, 1796	Sumpter, George, and Susanah Mayse.
Aug. 25, 1836	Sumpter, George, and Elizabeth Turner, dau. of Phoebe Turner.
May 17, 1792	Sumpter,William, and Margit Pyrtle.
May 4, 1818	Sutherland, George S. , and Patty Norman, dau. of William Norman.
Sept. 3, 1844	Suttenfield, James M. , and Nancy G. Taylor, dau. of Reuben Taylor.
Dec. 26, 1803	Sutton, Charles, and Nancy Watts.
Sept. 29, 1779	Tankersley, George, and Elizabeth Garrison.
Sept. 6, 1841	Taylor, Daniel G. , and Martha King, dau. of R. Taylor.
June 24, 1779	Taylor, George, and Hannah Jennings, dau. of Miles Jennings.
Jan. 24, 1811	Taylor, George, and Elizabeth McMillion.
Mar. 1, 1836	Taylor, George W. , and Sarah A. Hailey.
Jan. 13, 1845	Taylor, George W. , and Martha Ann Shelton.
Feb. 15, 1821	Taylor, German, and Ruth Smith.
Dec. 29, 1794	Taylor, James, and Elizabeth Williams.
Aug. 14, 1815	Taylor, James, and Martha Warham.
Dec. 18, 1838	Taylor, James L. , and Martha Jane Stults.
Sept. 18, 1837	Taylor, John, and Louisa M. Hankins.
Oct. 10, 1842	Taylor, John P. H. , and Ruth P. Baker, dau. of Catharine Baker.
Aug. 17, 1796	Taylor, William, and Sarah Worrell.
Nov. 10, 1817	Taylor, Wm. A. , and Catharine Hill.
Nov. 8, 1838	Taylor, William D. , and Julia Ann Lyell, dau. of Mary Ann Lyell.
Dec. 8, 1828	Terry, Abner R. , and Elenor Dyer.
Dec. 17, 1832	Terry, George, and Elizabeth Perkinson.
May 14, 1849	Terry, George, and Ruth Harriet Napier.

Oct. 11, 1799 Terry, Joseph, and Lucy Carter, consent of Barnet Carter.

Mar. 20, 1837 Terry, Joseph, and Pamelia Burch, dau. of Bazdel Burch.

Dec. 1, 1778 Thomas, Augustine, and Deborah Fulkerson, consent of Frederick Fulkerson.

July 13, 1812 Thomas, Edward, and Betsey Allen.

Dec. 8, 1817 Thomas, Joseph, and Ann Turner.

Jan. 27, 1814 Thomason, Adam, and Lucy Barns, dau. of James Barns.

Sept. 30, 1811 Thomason, Elias, and Eliza. Barns.

Nov. 7, 1826 Thomason, John, and Lucy Thomason.

July 27, 1801 Thomason, Joseph, and Hester Simpson.

Dec. 28, 1818 Thomason, Joseph, and Sarah Phifer.

Oct. 17, 1806 Thomasson, Arnold, and Pheby Dyer, dau. of George Dyer.

Dec. 7, 1827 Thomasson, Arnold, and Sarah Garthard, dau. of John Garthard, Sr.

Oct. 18, 1830 Thomasson, George D., and Elizabeth Pace.

Dec. 21, 1846 Thomasson, George, and Julia Ann Coleman.

Sept. 7, 1799 Thomasson, James, and Prudence Simpson.

Jan. 6, 1849 Thomasson, Presley, and Nancy Nunn.

Nov. 26, 1838 Thomasson, William, and Nancy B. Turner.

May 27, 1824 Thompson, Waddy, and Mary Abington, dau. of Henry Abington.

Mar. 12, 1794 Thompson, William, and Dolithear Stockton, dau. of Robert Stockton.

Aug. 30, 1826 Thornton, James, and Martha C. Royster, consent of Elizabeth Royster.

Sept. 17, 1838 Thrasher, John B., and Eliza Egan.

Nov. 14, 1781 Threlkeld, Elijah, and Elizabeth Cook.

May 4, 1805 Thurston, William, and Susanna Adams.

Sept. 21, 1846 Tinch, Andrew W., and Martha Jane Hardy, dau. of John Hardy.

May 10, 1842	Tio, William, and Matilda E. Sumpter.
Mar. 11, 1844	Tolbert, John J., and Liza McDaniel, consent of John McDonald.
Nov. 8, 1830	Toler, Wm. B., and Lucy Abington (born 26 Aug. 1809).
Apr. 11, 1807	Toombs, William, Jr., and Elizabeth Nickson, consent of William Nickson.
Oct. 31, 1797	Trahern, John, and Susannah Royster.
Jan. 9, 1815	Traylor, John C., and Tabitha Bailey.
Jan. 20, 1838	Traylor, Robert B., and Celia R. Mullins, dau. of Henry G. Mullins.
Mar. 27, 1820	Travis, Abner, and Rachel B. Weaver.
Dec. 8, 1834	Trent, James W., and Dorotha King.
Jan. 23, 1831	Turner, Aaron, and Texceney Bateman, dau. of Azel Bateman.
Jan. 9, 1824	Turner, Constantine, and Elizabeth Pyrtle.
Nov. 2, 1801	Turner, George, and Milly Stone.
June 29, 1830	Turner, Isaiah, and Elizabeth Gilley, consent of George Gilley.
Sept. 15, 1838	Turner, James O., and Sally Cahill, dau. of Perry Cahill.
Jan. 14, 1831	Turner, John, and Eliza Norman, dau. of Dutton Norman.
Sept. 14, 1836	Turner, Marlin, and Sally Long.
Dec. 13, 1841	Turner, Meadows, and Eliza Jane Griffith.
Dec. 9, 1822	Turner, Meshach, and Nancy Martin.
July 11, 1814	Turner, Pollard, and Eliza. Fifer.
Nov. 15, 1806	Turner, Shores, and Addelpa Turner, dau. of William Turner.
Dec. 3, 1828	Turner, Stephen T., and Nancy Gilley, dau. of George Gilley.
Sept. --, 1825	Turner, Thomas, and Caroline Pyrtle, dau. of John P. Pyrtle.
Nov. 15, 1843	Turner, Whitfield, and Sarah Ann Martin.
Dec. 14, 1812	Turner, William, and Pheba Wilson.

Jan. 10, 1814   Turner, William, and Elizabeth Heard.

Dec. 11, 1837   Turner, William, and Martha Philpott.

June 3, 1846   Tush, Lewis G., and Matilda Moore.

July 22, 1840   Tyree, John, and Nancy Thomasson, dau. of Joseph Thomasson.

Sept. 10, 1838 Uhles, David, son of Mary Uhles, and Martha Prewit, dau. of Elizabeth Prewit.

Feb. 6, 1827   Varnon, Myer, and Lucinda Martin.

Jan. 10, 1831   Varnum, Ewell, and Willie Oakley, dau. of John and Winey Oakley.

May 30, 1807   Vaughan, Aris, Jr., and Sarah Sands.

Aug. 16, 1802   Vaughan, Gabriel, and Nancy Pyrtle, sister of John P. Pyrtle.

Nov. 2, 1810   Vaughan, Robert, and Elizabeth Durham.

Aug. 17, 1801   Vaughan, William, and Jean Watson.

Oct. 5, 1816   Vawter, Chadwell, and Susannah Taylor, dau. of George Taylor, Sr.

Oct. 18, 1845   Vernon, James, and Sally Fisher.

Nov. 14, 1846   Vier, James, and Mary R. Baker, dau. of Catharine Baker.

Sept. 29, 1779 Wade, Moses, and Fanny Ferguson, dau. of Robt. Ferguson.

Nov. 28, 1796   Wade, Pierce, and Fereby Hutchings.

Nov. 14, 1846   Wade, William, and Jane Bowles.

June 24, 1845   Wagoner, Samuel H., consent of Daniel Wagoner, and Elizabeth Hundley.

Dec. 28, 1814   Walker, Arnold, and Elander Gravley.

Nov. 10, 1845   Walker, Joseph Logan, and Lucy G. Hix.

Oct. 25, 1802   Walker, William (of Pittsylvania Co.), and Frances Nunnelee.

Dec. 18, 1809   Walker, William S., and Salley Norman.

Nov. 11, 1811   Walker, William, and Polly Hendren.

Oct. 30, 1837	Wall, Joseph Henry, and Eliza Reed Grant, dau. of Archibald Grant.
Mar. 20, 1823	Waller, Edmund, and Ann King.
July 12, 1806	Waller, Carr, and Susanna Edwards.
July 10, 1806	Waller, George, Jr., and Polley Staples, dau. of John Staples.
Mar. 24, 1830	Waller, George, Jr., and Eliza Waller.
Jan. 7, 1822	Waller, Granvill, and Virginia McDonald.
Oct, 18, 1841	Waller, James E., and Mary Fontaine.
Feb. 8, 1803	Waller, William, and Polley Barksdale, dau. of Sarah Barksdale.
Sept. 1, 1841	Walton, Elisha, and Milley Stone.
Jan. 16, 1838	Walton, Pleasant, and Ruth Stone.
July 9, 1849	Warren, Balaam, and Julia A. Barber.
Nov. 4, 1807	Warren, Drury, and Salley Jameson.
Jan. 11, 1813	Warren, Jessee, and Elizabeth Stewart.
May 27, 1806	Warren, John, and Elizabeth Martin (?).
Mar. 11, 1840	Warren, Lemuel, and Emily Prewit, dau. of John Prewit.
Mar. 29, 1800	Warren, William, Jr., and Rosannah Parsley, dau. of Thomas Parsley.
Dec. 24, 1823	Warthen, Walter G., and Lucy A. Rea, consent of Mildred Rea.
Aug. 2, 1779	Wash, John, and Nancy Frazer Gatewood.
Feb. 29, 1836	Watkins, John D., and Jane A. G. Martin, dau. of Jos. Martin.
Sept. 11, 1844	Watkins, Peter W., and Louisa Hairston, dau. of Geo. Hairston.
Jan. 10, 1837	Watkins, Thomas H., and Letitia Hairston.
Sept. 1, 1798	Watkins, William, and Jemima Dickerson.
Oct. 14, 1809	Watson, David, and Sally Minter, dau. of John Minter.
Oct. 12, 1826	Watson, Davis, and Nancy Cayton, dau. of Cornelius Cayton.

Apr. 23, 1814   Watson, Henry D., and Sarah Waller.

June 18, 1800   Watson, John Wright, and Frances Pace, dau. of
Joel and Mary Pace.

----- --- 1845 Watson, Lewis, and Eliza C. Gibson, dau. of John Gibson.

Oct. 29, 1800   Watson, Mical, and Doshe Northcutt.

Apr. 11, 1839   Watson, Peerson, and Elizabeth Pruet.

Dec. 18, 1799   Watson, Stinson, and Tabitha Minter, dau. of John Minter.

May 15, 1831   Weaver, Benjamin, and Nancy Leake.

Aug. 10, 1837   Weaver, John, and Nancy Dorse.

Sept. 10, 1825   Weaver, Joseph C., and Sarah Leake.

Apr. 13, 1813   Webb (?), Robert, and Eliza. Thacker.

Nov. 11, 1816   Webb, Sylvester, and Elizabeth Jones.

Nov. 28, 1807   Webb, Thomas, and Elizabeth East.

Dec. 24, 1819   Weekly, Joseph (of Shenandoah County), and Elizabeth
Leake, dau. of Josiah Leake.

Sept. 6, 1780   Weir, John, and Margaret Lady, dau. of Christence Lady.

Feb. 18, 1795   Wells, Barna, and Salley Bayles.

Nov. 7, 1825   Wells, Edmond P., and Mary M. Hughes, consent of
Jamima Hughes.

Dec. 2, 1831   Wells, Edward, and America Griffin, dau. of
Richard Griffin.

Sept. 16, 1828   Wells, Francis, and Sarah Smith.

Dec. 19, 1801   Wells, George, and Susana King, dau. of George King.

Apr. 24, 1809   Wells, George R., and Nancy Pettey, consent of
Davis Pettey.

July 12, 1842   Wells, James M., and Frances Margaret Travis, consent
of Rachel B. Travis.

Dec. 14, 1846   Wells, John, and Matilda Wells.

Jan. 19, 1842   Wells, Peter W., and Susan Oakley.

Apr. 23, 1827   Wells, Reuben, and Patsy Rogers.

Oct. 31, 1818   Wells, Starling, and Martha Dillion.

Dec. 18, 1824   Wells, Thomas, and Milly Chishenhall.

July 24, 1828   Wells, William C., and Lucy A. Hughes.

May 14, 1842   Wells, William, and Mary A. Scrawyer.

Oct. 11, 1844   Wells, William Burwell, and Nancy Morris,
"widow of Benjamin Morris."

Dec. 26, 1792   Wheat, Benjamin, and Martha Chavis (?).

Apr. 24, 1795   White, Ambrose, and Sally Hudgins.

June 14, 1798   White, Richard, and Susanah Henry.

Aug. 18, 1845   Wightman, James E., and Jane Lee McBride.
John L. Lee, "uncle" of wife.

Nov. 9, 1846   Wightman, John T., and Eliza J. Nowlin, dau. of
Bryan W. Nowlin.

Oct. 31, 1836   Wilks, Josiah, and Margaret Spencer, dau. of Ruth
Spencer.

Apr. 30, 1811   Williams, Abraham, and Patsey Stults.

Oct. 21, 1836   Williams, Bird, and Mary Sampson, dau. of Sarah Sampson.

May 15, 1804   Williams, David, and Nancy Larimore.

Oct. 20, 1842   Williams, Elam, and Sally H. Waller, grdns. Polly
and John S. Waller.

Oct. 4, 1806   Williams, Ephriam, and Sally Hutchings.

Oct. 14, 1810   Williams, John, and Elizabeth Salmon.

Nov. 11, 1809   Williams, Joseph, and Sally Procter, dau. of Joshua Procter.

Feb. 27, 1797   Williams, Ozborne, and Salley Wade.

Oct. 11, 1841   Williams, Robert M., and Elizabeth P. Martin, dau.
of Jos. Martin.

Dec. 29, 1806   Williams, Thomas, and Jeany Davis.

Dec. 28, 1809   Williams, Thos., and Fanny Webb.

July 18, 1836   Williams, Thomas, and Elizabeth Mills, consent of
Francis Mills.

Apr. 11, 1839   Williams, William B., and Mary Ann Campbell, dau.
of John Campbell.

Sept. 18, 1793   Williamson, Robert, and Nancy Cox.

Dec. 27, 1802	Wills, Benjamin, and Susana Nixon.
Jan. 11, 1808	Wills, John, Jr., and Polley King.
Feb. 3, 1826	Wills, Richard, and Susan Davis.
Nov. 7, 1816	Wills, Thomas, and Bethenia King.
Dec. 20, 1845	Wilmoth, William, and Susan Thomas.
Apr. 6, 1841	Wilson, Andrew, and Betsey P. Moore, dau. of James Moore.
Feb. 25, 1829	Wilson, Aaron, Jr., and Sarah Jane Gilley, dau. of Joseph Gilley.
Dec. 11, 1835	Wilson, Bartlett, and Susan Hailey, dau. of Thomas Wilson.
Dec. 2, 1845	Wilson, Jackson D. M., and Rhoda V. Watson.
July 14, 1817	Wilson, James, and Mary Meakes, consent of Polly Roberts.
Feb. 2, 1814	Wilson, John, and Lucy Fortune (widow).
Nov. 7, 1821	Wilson, John, and Polly Key, consent of Dabney and Betsy Key.
Nov. 3, 1828	Wilson, John, and Ann Davis.
Oct. 7, 1840	Wilson, Morgan, and Martha Odle, dau. of George Odle.
Nov. 29, 1802	Wilson, Moses, and Elizabeth Hopper.
May 19, 1793	Wilson, Nathaniel, and Susannah Stephens, consent of Susannah and William Stevens.
Dec. 23, 1805	Wilson, Thomas, and Elly Wilson, dau. of James Wilson.
Nov. 25, 1836	Wilson, William, and Charrity Jones. Polly J. Norman (for wife).
Jan. 22, 1844	Wilson, William, and Sarah McDaniel.
Dec. 10, 1821	Wingfield, Charles M., and Sally W. Marshall, dau. of Dennis Marshall.
Dec. 20, 1825	Winn, Joseph, and Elizabeth Anderson.
Aug. 14, 1820	Winston, Edmund, and Eliza Louisa Fontaine.
Nov. 19, 1815	Witt, Daniel, and Martha Brewer.
Jan. 9, 1821	Wood, Moses, and Elizabeth M. Smith, dau. of Sally Smith.

Apr. 9, 1827   Woodall, Christopher T., and Margaret Simes.

June 25, 1815   Woodall, James, and Jane Shackelford.

Dec. 14, 1814   Woodall, Jessee, and Nancy Woodall, dau. of Samuel
and Joanah Woodall.

Feb. 17, 1778   Woods, George, and Faney Mason, dau. of Robert Mason.

Aug. 5, 1779   Woods, Hugh, and Sarahann George, dau. of Wm. George.

Apr. 10, 1782   Woods, John, and Lucy Hawkins.

Jan. 20, 1806   Woodson, Benjamin, and Patsey Leseuer, dau. of
Martel Leseuer.

Nov. 6, 1835   Woody, Allen, and Ann Williamson.

Dec. 7, 1830   Wootton, John T., and Lucy D. Redd, consent of
John Redd.

Aug. 28, 1816   Wootton, Thomas J., and Polina D. Trent.

Mar. 17, 1817   Wootton, William H., and Kitty B. Trent.

Feb. 17, 1826   Wray (or Rea), Bruce, and Polly Cox.

July 7, 1849   Wray, Chesley M., and Eliza J. Gearrett, consent of
John Gearrett.

Jan. 7, 1839   Wray, Samuel P., and Martha Suttonfield.

Dec. 16, 1823   Wright, Daniel O., and Elizabeth Pulliam, consent of
William Pulliam.

Nov. 13, 1834   Wright, James, and Lucy Goodman.

Nov. 10, 1823   Wyatt, Craven, and Elenor Richardson, consent only.

Dec. 6, 1836   Wyatt, Craven, and Nancy Eggleton, dau. of Thomas
Eggleton.

Nov. 14, 1844   Wyatt, Harrison, and Caroline Thomas, dau. of
Edward Thomas.

Dec. 14, 1816   Wyatt, Jno. P., and Aggatha Richardson, dau. of
Elijah Richardson.

Sept. 5, 1829   Wyatt, Saunders, and Rachel Delozier, consent of
Edward Delozier.

Nov. 28, 1845   Wyatt, Vincent, and Chancy Wyatt, dau. of Craven Wyatt.

Dec. 19, 1846   Wyatt, Wesley S., and Lubinda Thomas, dau. of
Edward Thomas.

Nov. 16, 1810   Young, David, and Nelly Humfreys, dau. of
                    Morris Humfreys.

May 10, 1830   -------, Simeon C., and Mary Amelia Tyson, grdn.
                    for husband.

INDEX

Abingdon
  Nancy - Major, James

Abington,
  Lucy - Toler, Wm. B.
  Mary - Thompson, Waddy

Acholas (?),
  Phebe - Griggs, John

Adams,
  Eleanor - Letchworth, Benjamin
  Susanna - Lansford, William
  Susanna - Thurston, William

Agee,
  Nancy L. - Forbes, John R.
  Polly - Peddigo, Moses

Akin,
  Jeanny - Burgess, Harrison
  Margaret - Nucum, Cary
  Mary - Roberts, John
  Sarah - Paul, John

Alexander,
  Betsey - Smith, Thomas
  Obedience - Gearhart, Peter

Allen,
  Betsey - Thomas, Edward
  Eliza D. - Mathews, James
  Elizabeth - Deshazo, Richard
  Gilley - Lawrence, Henry
  Mary - Francis, Matthew
  Mary J - Bird, Marshall
  Nancy - Carter, Edward
  Oney - Austin, John
  Susanna - Mills, William F.

Altick,
  Sally T. - Cooper, Greensville

Anderson,
  Dolly - Lindsey, Joshua
  Elizabeth - Odell, Joseph
  Elizabeth - Winn, Joseph
  Mary E. - Starling, Edmund T.

Anglin,
  Armine - Goolsby, Charles

Anthony,
  Agnes - Blakey, Churchill
  Jean - Gilliam, John B.

Arthur,
  Sarah - Earls, Thomas

Atkisson,
  Ruth - Mattock, William

Bailey,
  Charlotte - Allen, Pines
  Nancy - Odle, John
  Tabitha - Traylor, John C.

Baker,
  Frances - Price, Williamson E.
  Jamima - Baker, Thomas
  Lucinda T. - Craghead, Thomas L.
  Lucy - Simms, John D.
  Mary R. - Vier, James
  Ruth P. - Taylor, John P. H.

Barber,
  Coley - Goode, Thomas
  Julia A. - Warren, Balaam
  Nelly - Jones, John L.

Barker,
  Eliza - Nance, Pleasant
  Isbell - Dyer, Joel
  Martha - Childress, John
  Mary A. - Harville, George A.
  Nancy - Creasey, Henry
  Rena - Lemon (?), Jefferson
  Sarah - Barker, Gwilliams

Barksdale,
  Polley - Waller, William

Barns,
  Eliza. - Thomason, Elias
  Lucy - Thomason, Adam

Barrow,
  Cassandra - Jones, Armistead
  Elizabeth Jane - Hankins,
    James A.
  Julia - Arnold, James
  Mary H. - Stockton, Charles W.
  Susan E. - Stockton, William L.

Bassett,
　Eliza - Hopper, Allen
　Martha - Bassett, Burwell W.
　Martha - Dyer, John S.
　Mary Catharine - Hill, William W.
　Mary D. - Philpott, Charles

Bateman,
　Elizabeth - Creasy, William
　Sarah - Harris, Fuler
　Texceney - Turner, Aaron

Batty (?),
　Elizabeth - Grayham, Arthur

Bauldin,
　Balzora - Mitchell, Joel L.
　Jane - Duvall, Marine

Bayles,
　Salley - Wells, Barna

Bays,
　Elizabeth - Hopper, James

Beck,
　Emeline - Mann, George
　Lucy - Brown, Thomas

Bellama,
　Elizabeth - Hannah, Townley

Birchett,
　Hanna - Stanley, Thomas
　Sidney - Leffel, Thomas

Bird,
　Sally S. - Moorman, Edwin W.

Bishop,
　Elizabeth - Harris, Henry

Bocock,
　Frances Ann - Hensley, William
　Margaret - Bondurant, James
　Mary - Hardy, Curtis

Bolling,
　Fanny - Bowles, John
　Leanner - Cox, John

Bondurant,
　Sarah - Pemberton, Richard

Bottom,
　Maria Ann - Brewer, John S.

Bouldin,
　Amy G. - Payne, Thomas
　Ann P. - Lamkin, Richard G.
　Eliza C. - Crews, Gideon
　Francinia - Cheatham, Edmund
　Letty Ann - Payne, William
　Nancy - Alexander, Joseph
　Nancy - Egleton, George
　Nancy - Rowland, Washington
　Polly - Rowland, Gilbert
　Sally - Cobler, John

Bowles,
　Jane - Edwards, Williamson K.
　Jane - Wade, William

Bradberry,
　Tabitha W. - Eaton, Daniel

Bradley,
　Susan E. - Garrot, John

Brashears,
　Polly - Smith, Allen

Bray,
　Jane - Dodson, Josiah
　Unity - Golden, Andy

Brewer,
　Lucy - Scales, John
　Martha - Witt, Daniel
　Matilda - Rowland, Creed
　Sarah - Bird, Abner

Briant,
　Elizabeth - Gilley, Joseph

Briscoe,
　Milley - O'Neal, Basil

Brittain,
　Elizabeth - Edwards, William

Brock,
　Lucy Allen - Burnett, John

Brown,
  Lizey - Jamerson, William

Bryant,
  Adeline - Faris, George W.
  Matilda - Martin, Jesse G.
  Salley - Mahon, William

Burch,
  Pamelia - Terry, Joseph

Burchett,
  Ailsey - Agee, Jacob
  Lucy - Reynolds, William
  Martha - Maupin, Morgan
  Sarah - Kington, Reubin

Burgess,
  Dosha - Foster, James
  Elizabeth - Hefflinger, Jacob
  Mary - Minter, Othniel
  Polly - Mullin, David
  Mary D. - Minter, William L.

Burrus,
  Abigail - Kellam, Horatio

Burton,
  Hannah - McKenny, Henry

Bybee,
  Bettey - Kelly, John

Cahall,
  Eliza Jane - Bateman, John

Cahill,
  Diannah - Philpott, David
  Mary - King, George
  Mary E. - Price, James
  Nancy - Philpott, Zachariah
  Sally - Turner, James O.

Campbell,
  Mary Ann - Williams, William B.

Cannon,
  Caty - Melvin, James

Carter,
  Ann - Medley, John
  Delila - Dillon, Elison
  Eliza. - Moore, William
  Ethney Malinda - Fleeman,
    Hezekiah
  Lucy - Terry, Joseph
  Nancy - Payne, Robert

Carter, (cont.)
  Polly - Payne, Wryland
  Sarah - Bishop, William

Carver,
  Sally - Clarke, Thomas

Casey,
  Martha - Barnett, Thomas
  Polly - Mahon, Edmund

Cassady,
  Coatney - Palmer, Elijah

Cayton,
  Harriet - Gilley, Alfred
  Manurvey - Cox, William K.
  Matilda - Roach, James
  Nancy - Watson, Davis

Chandler,
  Polley - Slate, Isham

Chapman,
  Polley - Akin, Thomas

Chavis (?)
  Martha - Wheat, Benjamin

Cheatham,
  Elizabeth - Kennerly, John W.
  Jean - Athey, Benjamin
  Martha - Morriss, Archibald
  Tabitha - Morris, William

Cheeley,
  Harriett - Dyer, Fontaine
  Sarah - Pullin, Thomas

Cheeley (or Chily),
  Mary Ann - Neblett, William S.

Cheely,
  Cythia - Byington, Moses
  Elizabeth - Staples (or Stoops),
    John

Chessure,
  Nancy - Davis, Coleman
  Nancy - Higgs, William

Childress,
  Sarah - Petty, Davis M.

Chishenhall,
  Milly - Wells, Thomas

Chowning,
  Sarah - Kelley, Mason

Christian,
  Judith F. - Hickman, Benjamin T.
  Mary L. - Alison, Robert

Clanton,
  Ann - Prewit, Elijah
  Dolley - Pruitt, John
  Dorotha - Griggs, Peter F.
  Elizabeth - Perkins, Joseph
  Elizabeth - Philpott, Garrett
  Mary G. - Gravely, John K.
  Parthena - Pulliam, Drury

Clark,
  Elizabeth - Nunn, William
  Fidilia - Hodges, John
  Henrietta - Clark, John
  Jane - Clarke, John, Jr.
  Lidia - Gravley, William
  Lydia - Shoemate, Tollaver
  Martha Ann - Mitchell, Granville
  Martha W. - Smith, James M.
  Matilda - Gravley, George
  Nancy - Shoemake, James
  Ruth - Draper, John
  Sally V. - Nunn, Joel P.
  Susanna - Brown, Starling

Clarke,
  Franky - Nunn, Thomas
  Peggy - Oldham, William
  Sarah - Burton, William

Clift,
  Mary S. - Clemons, John

Clifton,
  Arrenia - Lewis, Deveroux

Clinkscales,
  Pemelia J. - Rea, Edmund J.
  Sophia - Hudson, Daniel

Cobb,
  Ann - Haney, Lewis

Cole,
  Harriet E. - Marshall, Reuben D.
  Sarah - Fontaine, Patrick Henry, Jr.

Coleman,
  Julia Ann - Thomasson, George
  Martha - Davis, Thomas B.
  Mary - Feazel, John M.
  Nancy - Hunter, John

Cook,
  Elizabeth - Threlkeld, Elijah

Cooper,
  Agnes - Hamilton, George
  Lucinda - Gravely, George
  Nancy - Heffelfinger,
    Greensville

Cothrin,
  Mary - Bridel, Enock

Coursey,
  Caty - Anglin, Samuel
  Nancy - Hailey, Barnaba

Cousins,
  America - Cousins, Henry M.
  Aggy - Mann, Benja.
  Ann - Artis, Jeff

Cox,
  Elizabeth - Cox, John
  Franky - Pulliam, William
  Janett - Larrison, Peter
  Margaret E. - Payne, Ryland
  Martha - Gilley, Samuel
  Milly - Land, Jachariah
  Nancy - Williamson, Robert
  Polly - Rea (or Wray),
    Bruce

Cradock,
  Polley - Mayner, Stephen

Craig,
  Julia - Jackson, James

Crawley,
  Prudence - Elliott, Joseph

Creacy (?),
  Phebe - Davis, William, Jr.

Creasey,
  Sally - Smith, Spenser

Creasy,
  Patsy - Smith, William

Crews,
  Susanna E. - Dallas, Bird

Crowley,
  Elizabeth - Compton, Arthemus

Cummins,
  Elenor - Simmons, Charles

Cunningham,
  Milly - Smith, Thomas

Custer,
  Elizabeth - Dyer, Jefferson

Dains (?),
  Nancy - Cunningham, Jos.

Dalton,
  Nancy - Nance, James

Dandridge,
  Eliza. Ann - Hereford,
    Dr. William
  Sarah T. - Starling, William H.

Daniel,
  Frances - Hardy, Thrashley

Davis,
  Ann - Wilson, John
  Chancy - Barrow, David
  Charlotte - Martin, George
  Elenor - Davis, Williamson
  Jeany - Williams, Thomas
  Lucy - Holland, Stephen
  Margaret - Minter, Joseph
  Margaret C. - Jones, Joseph M.
  Mary - Akin, Michael
  Mary - Craig, Thomas
  Mary C. - Ramsey, Woodson
  Nancy - Draper, Thomas
  Nancy - Garner, William
  Rachel - Kelly, John
  Sarah - Lewis, John
  Susan - Clowers, George W.
  Susan - Wills, Richard

Delozer,
  Elizabeth - Crane, Samuel
  Nancy - Stewart, Alexander
  Rhoda - Pearson, Meredith

Delozier,
  Rachel - Wyatt, Saunders

Dent,
  Elizabeth - Bradbury, James
  Susannah - Maupin, Jessee

Deshazo,
  Frances - Allen, Coleman
  Sarah - Pace, Francis
  Tabitha - Connaway, Robert

Devin,
  Susan C. - Hundley, Ambrose D.

Dickerson,
  Agatha - Lyell, Richard
  Catharine M. - Cheeley,
    Cuthbert
  Jemima - Watkins, William

Dickinson,
  Pocahontas - Grant, John H.

Dillard,
  Elizabeth - Christian,
    Capt. John
  Jeaney - Cheatham, Leonard, Jr.
  Jennett - Clinkscales, James
  Mary Waller - Spencer,
    David H.
  Nancy - Hogans, Wm.
  Ruth - Spencer, John
  Sarah S. - Hairston, Nicholas H.
  Sarah S. - Hughs, Madison R.

Dillen,
  Elizabeth - Philpott, John W.
  Mary - Carter, Harriss
  Nancy - Smith, Joseph
  Sarah - Phillips, Alexander

Dilliard,
  Elizabeth M. - Stone, Daniel

Dillingham,
  Ann - Dillingham, Lott
  Elizabeth - Norris, Ezebulon

Dillion,
  Ann - Cook, Alexander
  Elizabeth - Baker, George
  Elizabeth Mary - Edwards,
    Stephen
  Lucy - Gregory, William

Dillion (cont.),
  Martha - Wells, Starling
  Mary - Carter, Joseph
  Mary - Pettit, John
  Nancy - Spencer, John
  Ruth - Burriss, Jacob
  Susan - Gyer, Joseph
  Susanah - Officer, Thomas

Dillon,
  Elizabeth - Carter, Cary
  Judith - Bradberry, Richard

Dix,
  Ann - Houston, David G.

Dorse,
  Nancy - Weaver, John

Dorson,
  Sally - Bocock, Drury

Doyle,
  Agnes - Leak, Dabney F.
  Harriett - Leake, Garland
  Mary Ann - Minter, Richard W.

Draper,
  Frances - Bird, Lewis
  Lucy - Draper, William
  Ruth - Dyer, Hugh

Dunavant,
  Eliza Ann - Marshall, John W.
  Sarah - Smith, David

Dunlap,
  Sarah - Patrick, James

Dunn,
  Catherine - Briscoe, Truman
  Nancy - Meaks, Calvin W.

Durham,
  Elizabeth - Vaughan, Robert

Duvall,
  Elvira - Carter, Cary

Dyer,
  Elenor - Terry, Abner R.
  Martha - Gravly, Lewis
  Martha - Spencer, Nathaniel
  Mary - Martin, Bailey

Dyer (cont.)
  Pheby - Thomasson, Arnold
  Rachel - Jones, Greenwood

Eanes,
  Mary Jane - Daulton, James

East,
  Elizabeth - Fowler, William
  Elizabeth - Webb, Thomas
  Nancy - Forbes, Austin
  Sally - Bouldin, Richard T.

Easter,
  Milley - Steward, William

Eckhols,
  Laura - Jackson, James H.

Edmundson,
  Salley - Cockram, Wm.

Edwards,
  Louisa - Nunn, Stephen
  Lucy - Cason, Edward
  Martha - Hundley, Hiram B.
  Martha M. - Fernenho, Milton
  Mary - Bowles, John
  Mary - Burch, Basil
  Susan C. - Lacy, Charles H.
  Susanna - Waller, Carr

Egan,
  Eliza - Thrasher, John B.

Eggleton,
  Jane - Mathews, Claiborne
  Jane A. - Minter, Silas
  Martha - Compton, James
  Mildred - Mathews, Coleman
  Nancy - Wyatt, Craven

Egleton,
  Lucy - Stults, Joseph

Elliott,
  Susanna - Gaulding, Moses

Epperson,
  Tabitha C. - Marshall, William

Estis,
  Mariah - Barber, Carter

Evins,
  Mary - Petty, Isham M.

Farguson,
  Fanny - Wade, Moses
  Jean - Alexander, William

Faris,
  Sally - Aistrop, Oliver P.

Fariss (or Pharis),
  Betsy G. - Jennings, Swafford W.

Farriss,
  Nancy - Farriss, Archabald, Jr.
  Patty - Penn, George

Fearney,
  Polly - Martin, William

Feazle,
  Caleniece - Coleman, James
  Elizabeth B. - Bradberry, Peter
  Rachel - Archer, Joseph

Fee,
  Dicey - Means, Thomas P.
  Jane - Stephens, Coleman

Fifer,
  Eliza. - Turner, Pollard
  Martha - Pease, Edward
  Polly - Gessett, Cavin

Fisher,
  Sally - Vernon, James

Fleeman,
  Betsey - Hodges, Obediah

Fleemon,
  Mary J. - Richardson, Arthur
  Polley - Egleton, Thomas

Fontaine,
  Eliza Louisa - Winston, Edmund
  Martha - Dandridge, Nathaniel
    West, Jr.
  Martha - Redd, Overton
  Martha A. - Anderson, Leonard W.
  Martha H. - Perkins, William, Sr.
  Mary - Perkins, Jesse
  Mary - Waller, James E.
  Sarah Ann - Redd, Edmund B.

Fortune,
  Lucy - Wilson, John
  Maria - Estes, Jesse
  Sarah Ann - Dyer, James

Foster,
  Elizabeth - Foster, John

France,
  Matilda - Burgess, John
  Sarah - Colley, John

Francis,
  Judia - Rea, James

Franklin,
  Fanny - Rea, Wilson

Franklyn,
  Susannah - Glass, Benjm.

Fulkerson,
  Deborah - Thomas, Augustine
  Mary - Hill, Amannuel

Gardner,
  Jamima - Knox, Benjamin

Garner,
  Healin - Letcher, James
  Judith - Sanford (or Sandford),
    John

Garrison,
  Elizabeth - Tankersley,
    George

Garthard,
  Sarah - Thomasson, Arnold

Gates,
  Hannah - Salmon, Hezekiah

Gatewood,
  Nancy Frazer - Wash, John

Gearrett,
  Eliza J. - Wray, Chesley M.

George,
  Mary - Jones, Willis
  Nancy - Dyer, George
  Pegy - Bledsoe, Peachy
  Sarah - Bush, Henry
  Sarahann - Woods, Hugh

Gibson,
    Eliza C. - Watson, Lewis

Gilbert,
    Sarah - Aistrop, John

Gilley,
    Caroline M. - Odle, William W.
    Elizabeth - Turner, Isaiah
    Levina - Bateman, Azel
    Lucy - Bundurant, John
    Lucy - Griggs, Peter
    Mary - Cobb, Nelson
    Mary - Gilley, Leftwich
    Mary - Gilley, William
    Mary - Mahon, Willis
    Nancy - Mabe, Reubin
    Nancy - Turner, Stephen T.
    Rachel - Davis, Israel
    Salley - Gilley, Burwell
    Sarah Jane - Wilson, Aaron, Jr.
    Sereney - Odle, James
    Unity - Stratton, James

Gilly,
    Nancy - Cox, William
    Patsy - Cox, Bennett

Gilpin,
    Amy - Mullins, Thomas

Going,
    Elizabeth - Miner, Heyekiah
    Elizabeth - Moore, Charles

Good,
    Elizabeth - Edwards, James M.

Goode,
    Catherine - Bowles, Alexander H.
    Mary - Draper, William F.
    Sally - Oxley, Alfred

Goodman,
    Elizabeth - McDaniel, James
    Lucy - Wright, James
Gordon,
    Elizabeth - Staples, Norman

Grant,
    Eliza R. - Critenden, James
    Eliza Reed - Wall, Joseph Henry
    Jemima Vincent - Nance, Fontaine
    Mary Rebecca - Bateman, George

Graveley,
    Mary - Murphy, Peyton

Gravely,
    Eleanor - Dunigan, Thomas E.
    Eliza Ann - Rice, John D.
    Judith - Riddle, Ephriam
    Judith N. - Hix, William N.
    Mary F. - Peters, Dr. Henry D.
    Polley - Dyer, Benjamin
    Rachel Ann - Cheatham,
        Edmund B.
    Susannah - Clarke, Isaac

Graves,
    Ann - Parberry, James
    Elizabeth - Anderson, Robert

Gravley,
    Elander - Walker, Arnold
    Ellenor - Moore, William

Griffin,
    America - Wells, Edward
    Elizabeth - Fleeman, John
    Patsy - Jenkins, Joseph

Griffith,
    Eliza Jane - Turner, Meadows

Grigg,
    Gincy - Arthur, David

Griggs,
    Rebeccah - Burgess,
        Pendleton
    Sarah - Gover, William

Grogan,
    Letty - Kelley, Thomas
    Sally - Smith, James

Gunn,
    Zilpha - Elston, James

Gunnell,
    Elizabeth Letcher - Hill,
        Manning
    Nancy - Martin, Abraham

Hailey,
   Sarah A. - Taylor, George W.
   Susan - Wilson, Bartlett

Hairston,
   America - Callaway, John
   Elizabeth - Rowland, Michael
   Elizabeth - Seawell, John T.
   Elizabeth P. - Dillard,
     Dr. Peter F.
   Letitia - Watkins, Thomas H.
   Louisa - Watkins, Peter W.
   Ruth - Hairston, Peter
   Sarah - Rowland, Baldwin
   Susan - Martin, William

Hale,
   Sally - Armistead, Francis

Haley,
   Catharine - Richardson, James
   Joyce - Proctor, Lewis
   Lucy - Northcutt, Francis

Hamilton,
   Susannah - Richards, Shadrick

Hancock,
   Ann - Stewart, David

Hankins,
   Ann S. - Austin, Jefferson
   Eliza. J. - Austin, Garland A.
   Louisa M. - Taylor, John
   Lucy - Bray, John
   Martha L. - Gravely, Jabez L.
   Mary A. - Austin, Daniel B.
   Susannah - Clift, William
   Temperance - Hall, John

Hardy,
   Bethenia - Pace, Thomas
   Caty - Maupin, William
   Martha Jane - Tinch, Andrew W.
   Nancy - Bradbury, Mark

Harger,
   Martha - Briant, James

Harris,
   Agnes - Goodman, David
   Cyntha - Jones, Daniel
   Lucy W. - Price, John
   Mary Ann - Cox, Peter C.
   Salley - Green, James
   Virginia E. - Mahon, Reuben

Harriss,
   Nancy - Gray, Thomas

Harvey,
   Nancy Drucilla - Dyer, Joab

Hatcher,
   Marial - Crews, Samuel
   Polley - Shelton, Nathan
   Susanah - Durham, William

Hawkins,
   Lucy - Woods, John

Hay,
   Mary Ann - Athy, James

Hayse,
   Mary Ann - Ray, Joseph

Heard,
   Ann - Mitchell, Robert
   Elizabeth - Turner, William
   Mary - Davis, Peter
   Nancy - Davies, Benjamin
   Rosey - Meredith, William
   Sarah - Maghee, Martin

Hefflefinger,
   Hamar (?) - Barger, Peter
   Hanah - Pace, John

Hendren,
   Polly - Walker, William

Henry,
   Susanah - White, Richard

Henslee,
   Jeaney - Salmon, Noah

Hensley,
   Ava - Lyell, Richard
   Phebee - McKinney, Kinney
   Polly - Hardy, Thrashly
   Sally - Smith, Benjm.

Hensly,
   Patsy - Clark, Jonathan

Hereford,
   Jane - Leake, Andrew J.
   Jane - Payne, Robert

Herndon,
   Saley - Adams, Randolph

Hewlett,
    Elizabeth - Rea, James
    Joanna - Davis, Robert
    Nancy D. - Edwards, Chiles
    Polly - Gilley, Francis

Hibbert,
    Polley - Fifer (or Phifer),
        Bradley
    Sarah - Hardy, Owen

Hibbs,
    Rachel - Hunter, George

Hicks,
    Elizabeth - Lanier, Washington
    Nancy - Lester, Daniel

Higgs,
    Nancy - Loyd, Thomas
    Polly - Graveley, Joseph

Hill,
    Catharine - Taylor, Wm. A.
    Elizabeth - Brim, Nicholas
    Elizabeth - Harris, Joseph
    Elizabeth M. - Smith, Abner
    Judia - Hill, Jno. W.
    Lucinda S. - Pritchett, Richard H.
    Martha M. - Joyce, Thomas
    Matilda W. - Mullins, Henry G.
    Mildred F. - Hopper, Ezekiah
    Patsy - Dillard, George S.
    Ruth - Bernard, Walter
    Salley - Spencer, William

Hind,
    Elizabeth - Murfry, James

Hirston,
    Mary - Smith, Gideon

Hix,
    Elizabeth M. - Davis, Benjamin
    Lucy G. - Walker, Joseph Logan

Hodges,
    Mary - Fleming, Hodges

Holmes,
    Anna - Mastin, John
    Elizabeth - Salmon, Thadeus

Holt,
    Lucy Jane - Mitchell, Ignatius F.
    Pamelia - Phariss, George W.

Hooker,
    Ann - Moore, Shallen (or
        Stratton)

Hopper,
    Ailcey - Compton, Ebenazer
    Elizabeth - Grogan, Francis
    Elizabeth - Wilson, Moses
    Mary G. - Gilley, Joseph
    Nancy - Anderson, Seward G.

Hord,
    Ruth - Greenlee, James
    Salley - Greenlee, Ephriam M.

House,
    Caroline - McClane, Wm.

Hudgins,
    Sally - White, Ambrose

Hughes,
    Elizabeth - Cahall, Edward
    Leticia - Reamey, James
    Lucy A. - Wells, William C.
    Mary M. - Gravely, George
    Mary M. - Wells, Edmond P.
    Nancy W. - Allen, Pines
    Sarah M. - Nance, Stephen

Humfreys,
    Nelly - Young, David

Humphreys,
    Rachel - Sprouse, David

Humphrys,
    Sally - Long, Gabriel

Hundley,
    Elizabeth - Wagoner,
        Samuel H.
    Lucy - Bryant, Elisha

Hundly,
    Sarah - Richman, William H.

Hunt,
    Betsy - Jones, Willis
    Frances - Parish, Allen
    Lucy - Jones, Willis
    Matilda - Stokes, German

Hunter,
    Betsey - Bays, Jesse
    Caroline M. - Pace, James B.

Hunter (cont.),
    Elizabeth - Mathews, William
    Jeany - Bays, Isaiah
    Martha - Greenlee, David
    Milley - Pennell, John
    Patty - Spencer, George
    Polly - Bassett, Burrell

Hurd,
    Margaret - Pyrtle, Carr

Huston,
    Hesey - Jameson, Thomas

Hutchings,
    Fereby - Wade, Pierce
    Sally - Williams, Ephriam

Jackson,
    Bethena H. - Curtis, Elisha B.
    Nancy - Fuller, Brittain
    Nancy - Haley, William

Jamerson,
    Betsy H. - Smith, John

Jameson,
    Salley - Warren, Drury

Jarrett,
    Mary - Mills, Robert Wiley

Jarviss,
    Eliza. - Deshaure, Elijah
    Nancy - Pleasted (?), Joshua

Jennings,
    Hannah - Taylor, George

Johnson,
    Martha - Edwards, John
    Pamelia A. - Fishback, William

Johnston,
    Lucy - Riddle, Thomas
    Martha - Lawrence, James
    Sarah - Bray, John

Jones,
    ---- - Lovell, Markham
    Charrity - Wilson, William
    Delilah - Creasey, Joseph
    Eliza - Gregory, William

Jones (cont.),
    Elizabeth - Kyle, James
    Elizabeth - Montgomery, John
    Elizabeth - Sneed, Alexander
    Elizabeth - Webb, Sylvester
    Jamima - Standifore, Wm.
    Jane - Martin, Abner
    Louisa - Stokes, Allen
    Louisianna - Harris, James
    Lucy - Dickson, Jeremiah
    Martha J. - Burgess, John W.
    Mary - Martin, Orson
    Nancy - Anderson, Robert
    Nancy - Ford, Andrew
    Pamelia - Menzies, John C.
    Patsy - Allen, William
    Pitsey B. - Barber, Seth
    Polly - Daulton, William
    Rachel - Holt, Pascal
    Susannah - Griffith, William
    Susannah - Meeks, Coleman
    Winfred - Barber, Carter
    Winney - Alexander, Martin

Joy,
    Polly - Roberts, Lewis

Kelley,
    Caty - Parks, Joseph

Kelly,
    Lucy - Gilley, Francis

Kennon,
    Polley - Smith, Daniel

Key,
    Polly - Wilson, John

King,
    Ann - Jones, George
    Ann - Steagall, Alfred
    Ann - Waller, Edmund
    Bethenia - Wills, Thomas
    Betsey - Joyce, Andrew
    Charity - Davis, Samuel
    Dorotha - Trent, James W.
    Elizabeth - King, Lewis G.
    Elizabeth J. - Barrow,
      William M.
    Faney - McCullough, James
    Frances - Finney, John

King (cont.),
  Frances - Lester, Thomas
  Helen - Gravely, Joseph
  Jane - Pace, Daniel
  Martha - Taylor, Daniel G.
  Nancy - Howard, James
  Polley - Jones, Charles
  Polley - Wills, John, Jr.
  Polly W. - Nance, Peyton
  Sally - Griggs, Ira
  Sally L. - Cooper, Hubert
  Susan - Gregory, John
  Susan W. - Griggs, Wesley
  Susana - Wells, George
  Tabitha - Degraffenreid,
    Francis

Kitchen,
  Sarah - Stanley, Joseph

Lady,
  Margaret - Weir, John

Land,
  Mary - Chessure, Coleman

Lane,
  Nancy - Davis, Brice
  Rhody - Hopper, Terrell
  Salley - Nichols, Thomas
  Virginia - Marshall, Madison

Lanier,
  ----- - Burgess, Davis
  Elizabeth - Graves, Thomas
  Louisa - Price, Isaac B.
  Lucy - Ragsdill, Thomas
  Mary - Hill, Robert S.
  Nancy - Shelton, Leroy
  Susan - Dillon, William

Lansford,
  Susanna - Reynolds, George

Larason,
  Elizabeth - Key, Dabney

Larimore,
  Nancy - Williams, David

Larrison,
  Caty - Norman, Dutton
  Mary - Covington, William

Law,
  Averilla - Law, David F.
  Julian - Minter, Williamson

Lawless,
  Sally - Leake, Robert

Lawrence,
  Deborah - Lyell, Robert
  Ferbe - Perkinson, William
  Rayney - Law, James B.
  Sarah - Martin, Charles F.

Leake,
  Anna - Farris, Archibald
  Elizabeth - Weekly, Joseph
  Lucinda - Scales, Peter
  Nancy - Weaver, Benjamin
  Sarah - Weaver, Joseph C.

Lemmons,
  Eliza - Price, Zaid W.
  Virginia - Barker, Joseph

Lemon,
  Jane - Hopper, John

Leseuer,
  Patsey - Woodson, Benjamin

Lester,
  Susan - Richardson, John

Lesueur,
  Polley - Jones, Ambrose

Letcher,
  Parthenia - Pannell, David

Lewis,
  Anne - Dunn, James D.
  Mary - Robertson, John C.

Long,
  Disey - Humphreys, Morriss, Jr.
  Nelly - Fee, Henry
  Sally - Turner, Marlin

Lovell,
  Emblem M. - Hundley, George

Lovin,
  Mary - Dougherty, Samuel

Lucas,
  Elizabeth - Earles, Joshua

Lyell,
  Elizabeth Dalton - Jones, Thomas
  Emily - Hundley, Josiah
  Julia Ann - Taylor, William D.
  Nancy - Hunley, William

Lyle,
  Salley - Cary, William

Mabe,
  Sarah - Mason, David

Mahon,
  Arminda - Stratton, William Jackson

Marr,
  Sally J. - Hardeman, Constant

Marshall,
  Casandra A. - Clarke,
    William H.
  Eliza - Kellum, William
  Martha Harper - Conway, Benjm.
  Mary B. - Hagood, Anderson M.
  Sally W. - Wingfield, Charles M.

Martin,
  Ann - Clark, William
  Ann - Dillard, John H.
  Clarissa - Richardson, George
  Edda - Clark, Willis
  Elizabeth - Warren, John
  Elizabeth P. - Williams,
    Robert M.
  Hannah - Jones, Buckner
  Jane - Massey, James Adison
  Jane A. G. - Watkins, John D.
  Jane E. - Barding, John M.
  Jean - Peck, David
  Lucinda - Pyrtle, Barton
  Lucinda - Varnon, Myer
  Mary M. - Staples, John C.
  Matilda M. - Hairston, George S.
  Mourning - Clark, James
  Nancy - Arnn, Henry
  Nancy - Turner, Meshach
  Polly - Hughes, Ruben
  Sally - Armistead, Samuel
  Sally - Dillard, Overton R.
  Sarah Ann - Turner, Whitfield

Martin (cont.),
  Susan - Cook, Major Robert
  Susan Elizabeth - Stone, James M.
  Susanah - Burruss, Jacob
  Susanna - King, George

Mason,
  Faney - Woods, George

Masters,
  Polly - Eadens, John

Mathews,
  Edey - Gravely, Booker
  Kezia - Fleemon, Joseph
  Martha A. - Dalton, John A. B.
  Sophia W. - Shackleford, Wm.

Matthews,
  Lucy - Matthews, Dabney W.
  Rebecca - Pearson, James

Mauldin,
  Nancy - Burchett, Bartlett

Maupin,
  Elizabeth - Salmon, James D.
  Frances - Meredith, Elijah
  Lucy - Purdy, Anderson
  Sarah - Parsley, William

Mays,
  Nancy L. - Moore, Wm. B.

Mayse,
  Susanah - Sumpter, George

McBride,
  Elizabeth - Davis, William
  Jane Lee - Wightman, James E.
  Polly - Meredith, John

McCullock,
  Bettsey - Beck, Levy
  Mary - Shields, James

McCullough,
  Delilah - Grigg, Joseph W.
  Nancy - Hunt, John

McDaniel,
  Catharine - Marshall,
    Whittington
  Jane - Barker, Burwell

McDaniel (cont.),
  Liza - Tolbert, John J.
  Mary - Lemons, William
  Sarah - Millner, Thomas B.
  Sarah - Wilson, William

McDaniel (or McDonalld),
  Lavinia - Higgs, Samuel

McDonald,
  Dilly - Land, Nelson
  Elizabeth - Penn, Peter P.
  Virginia - Waller, Granvill

McKinzey,
  Delilah - Hemming, William

McMillion,
  Elizabeth - Smith, William
  Elizabeth - Taylor, George
  Polly - Edwards, James

Meade,
  America Ann - Singleton,
    William

Meakes,
  Mary - Wilson, James

Melvin,
  Ann - Stults, John
  Eliza. - Mastin, Jacob
  Mary - Smith, Dabney

Menefee,
  Nanny - Carter, Joseph

Meredith,
  Ann - Roberts, James
  Casah - Gear, Reubin
  Elizabeth - Dillen, James
  Lucy - Draper, William
  Lucy - Hutchison, John C.
  Mary - Heard, William
  Nancy - Burchett, Lenord
  Sidney - Haily, James
  Susannah - Burchett, Thos.

Miller,
  Keturiah - Cole, Samuel M.
  Lucy - Dix, Thomas
  Mary - Alexander, Robert
  Nancy - Fontaine, Patrick H.
  Nancy - Mayner, Jeremiah
  Rebecca - Perkins, William

Mills,
  Elizabeth - Williams, Thomas
  Icypeana - Oakley, William M.
  Jane S. - Floyd, William P.
  Louisa - Poindexter, John
  Malinda - Clark, Absalom
  (Martha) - Fry, Archilus
  Martha - Mills, William
  Parthenia E. - Anglin, Philip
  Rebecca - Dunivant, James

Minter,
  Betsey - Griggs, Michael
  Delila - Haily, Gabriel
  Elizabeth - Doyle, William M.
  Elizabeth A. - Cheshier, Thomas
  Franciana - Delozier, Perin
  Lucy B. - Smith, Daniel D.
  Mariah G. - Nunn, George W.
  Milley - Bell, Nathan
  Nancy - Fariss, William W.
  Nancy - Richardson, Abner
  Sally - Watson, David
  Sintha - Burch, James
  Susan F. - Allen, Jones
  Susannah - Stults, Thomas
  Tabitha - Harvell, Merritt
  Tabitha - Watson, Stinson

Mitchell,
  Elizabeth J. - Norman,
    Courtney W.
  Lethia Ann - Stone, Joseph P.
  Nancy - King, William

Molin,
  Nelly - Belleman, William

Montgomery,
  Eliza - Miles, Lawson H.

Moon,
  Elizabeth - Manning, Samuel

Moore,
  Betsey P. - Wilson, Andrew
  Biddy - Price, Allen
  Biddy - Rea, John B.
  Elizabeth - Aistrop, Robert G.
  Elizabeth - Mason, Carter W.
  Jane - Sigmon, William B.
  Jean - Harbour, John
  Lucinda - Price, Rece
  Malinda - Floyd, Benjamin H.

Moore,
  Matilda - Tush, Lewis G.
  Salley - Mills, Francis

Morris (or Norris),
  Jean - Davis, Williamson

Morris,
  Mary H. - Stegall, Richard W.
  Nancy - Wells, William Burwell
  Narcissa - Shelton, Joseph A.
  Sarah Ann - Carter, Dr. William

Morrison,
  Elizabeth B. - Galloway, James S.

Morriss,
  Lucy - Garrott, Gideon
  Nancy - Brewer, William

Morton,
  Judith - Edwards, Owen

Mullins,
  Ceally - Allen, Robert
  Celia R. - Traylor, Robert B.
  Lucy - Mathews, Calvin
  Margaret - Easter (or Esther),
    Wiley
  Milley - Beheler, John
  Susan - Mathews, Tandey
  Tibitha - Martin, Joshua

Munroe,
  Lucy - Hibbert, William
  Sidney - Philpott, John

Murfry,
  Ona (?) - Gilley, Peter

Murphy,
  Lucy - Dilliner, Henry
  Mary - Dent, Shadrick
  Susana - Meredith, Joseph

Nance,
  Bettsey - Nance, Allen
  Nancy - Marshall, Benjamin
  Sally - Samms, Elijah
  Sarah - Philpott, David
  Susanah - McCullock, Alexander
  Tabitha - Shackleford, Daniel

Napier,
  Gilley C. - Koger, John
  Ruth Harriet - Terry, George

Nicholds,
  Caroline Matilda, Dandridge,
    Thos. B.

Nickson,
  Elizabeth - Toombs,
    William, Jr.

Nicolds,
  Rhoda Virginia - Staples, James

Nixon,
  Susana - Wills, Benjamin

Norman,
  Eliza - Turner, John
  Elizabeth O. - Shelton,
    Thomas S.
  Lucinda - Cousins, Francis M.
  Mary J. - Fretwell, William
  Nancy - Larrison, James
  Nancy - Minter, Joseph
  Patty - Sutherland, George S.
  Salley - Walker, William S.
  Sarah O. - Mitchell, Archibald W.
  Sarah W. - Holland, William
  Virginia - Creasy, James

Norris (or Morris),
  Jean - Davis, Williamson

Norriss,
  Eliza. - Murphy, James
  Elizabeth - Lark, Robert

Northcutt,
  Doshe - Watson, Mical
  Elizabeth - Cheely,
    Cuthburth

Nowlin,
  Eliza J. - Wightman, John T.
  Martha C. - Fontaine,
    Charles H.

Nunn,
  Elizabeth - Alexander, Ingram
  Elizabeth - Dillen, William
  Elizabeth - Ramsey, Lacy
  Elizabeth - Stone, William
  Frances - Bowles, Lewis
  Jane - Feazle, Joab
  Mariah G. - Mills, James B.
  Mary - Cooper, Alexander
  Mary - Hollandsworth,
    Thomas
  Nancy - Thomasson, Presley

Nunnelee,
 Frances - Walker, William

Oakes,
 Eliza. - Nance, Terrell
 Polly - Goodwin, Joseph, Jr.
 Rachel - Cayton, William

Oakley,
 Milley - Evans, James
 Salley - Craig, William
 Susan - Wells, Peter W.
 Willie - Varnum, Ewell

Oaks,
 Polly - Norman, Nelson

Odaniel,
 Polly - Lovell, William

Odle,
 Elizabeth - Carter, George
 Louisa - Hundley, Granville
 Martha - Flanagan, Burwell
 Martha - Wilson, Morgan
 Matilda - Ragin, John
 Nancy - Flanigan, Beverly
 (alias Price)

Oldham,
 Winny - Clanton, Macklan

Pace,
 Dosha - Egelton, Thomas
 Elizabeth - Moore, Alexander
 Elizabeth - Shumate, Daniel
 Elizabeth - Thomasson,
 George D.
 Frances - Watson, John Wright
 Jean - Nunn, Thomas
 Lucinda T. - Stovall, James R.
 Lucy - Burgess, David
 Milly - Baker, Jeremiah
 Nancy - Hardy, Joseph
 Nancy - Shumate, Samuel
 Salley - Hunter, Samuel
 Sarah - Dillen, Jefferson

Pankey,
 Kesiah - Quimby, William

Parsley,
 Pheby - Poston, Edward
 Rachel - Hardy, Charles
 Rosannah - Warren, William, Jr.

Payne,
 Elizabeth - East, John
 Lettice - Chowning, John
 Lucindy - Hill, Thomas
 Lucy - Patterson, Jarrott
 Mildred - East, Joseph
 Polly - Hewlett, John

Pearson,
 Elizabeth - Lawrence, James H.
 Polly - Lawrence, Arthur F.
 Luticia - Johnson, William

Peddigo,
 Elizabeth - Dawson, John
 Sally - Griggs, Michael
 Sarah - Hardy, John

Pedigo,
 Amey - Parsley, William
 Betsey - Norriss, Samuel
 Lavina A. - Nunn, Josiah W.

Pedigoe,
 Mary - Elkins, David

Pelphry,
 Elizabeth - Quarles, James
 Sarah - Hannah, Alexander

Penn,
 Sarah - Norton, John

Perdie,
 Susannah - Rogers, William

Peregoy,
 Ruth - Murphy, Gabriel

Pergusson,
 Polly - Garthart, John

Perkins,
 Elley - Stephen, Lyon
 Mary - Cormick, Capt.
 Lewis M.

Perkinson,
  Elizabeth - Terry, George
  Lucy - Burch, John
  Patsey - Griggs, Michael
  Patsy - Fleeman, George

Pettey,
  Nancy - Wells, George R.

Pharis, (or Fariss),
  Betsy G. - Jennings, Swafford W.

Phifer,
  Sarah - Thomason, Joseph

Philips,
  Catharine - Doss, John

Phillips,
  Polly - Sandifer, Abraham

Phillpot,
  Casandra - Clark, Henry
  Elizabeth - Carter, Jessee
  Sarah - Raynolds, John
  Sarah Hanna - Smith, James

Philpott,
  Ann Garrett - Hollandsworth,
    Brice
  Betsey - Minter, Silas
  Caroline - Morris, William B.
  Elizabeth Jones - Phifer, John
  Eurelia (?) - Bird, James
  Hannah - Arnold, Lewis
  Martha - Carter, Fleming
  Martha - Turner, William
  Mary - Stone, John
  Mary Ann - Philpott, Allen
  Mary D. - Morris, Woodson
  Mary J. - Abington, William M.
  Nancy - Carter, John
  Patsy - Stone, Wm.
  Susannah - Perkinson, Hezekiah
  Susannah - Phifer, Forrest

Phyfer,
  Nancy - Philpott, John

Pigg,
  Sally - Dillion, William

Pleaster,
  Eliza H. - McMillion, John

Poindexter,
  Judith - Mills, Richard

Posten,
  Charity - Peddigo, John

Poston,
  Hopey - Simpson, Sanford
  Malinda - Peddigo, Henry
  Sarah - Pedigo, Elijah

Powers (alias Haffelfinger),
  Catharine - Heffelfinger, Henry

Pratt,
  Lucy - Price, John
  Michy - Brim, David
  Nancy - Sams, John

Prewit,
  Emily - Warren, Lemuel
  Martha - Uhles, David

Price,
  Lucy - Noe, Gideon
  Lucy W. - Norman, James B.

Prilliman,
  Baberry - Snidow, Philip

Procter,
  Sally - Williams, Joseph

Pruet,
  Elizabeth - Watson, Peerson

Pruette,
  Mary J. - Booth, George

Pulliam,
  Elizabeth - Wright, Daniel O.
  Polly - Parish, Lee
  Sarah - Covington, John

Pullium,
  Harriet - Curry, William

Pullom,
  Nancy - Cayton, Martin

Pursell,
  Elizabeth - Agee, William

Pyrtle,
  Anna - Cahill, Peregrin
  Caroline - Turner, Thomas
  Doratha - Martin, Early
  Elizabeth - Turner, Constantine
  Josephine - Shumate, Westley
  Lucy - Doss, Noah
  Margaret - Philpott, Samuel
  Margit - Sumpter, William
  Mary - Cunningham, William
  Nancy - Vaughan, Gabriel
  Sidny - Smith, Charles

Quarles,
  Dosha - Burnett, William
  Judith - Farris, Thomas
  Milley - Oakley, William

Radford,
  Milly - Rowland, William

Ramey,
  Nancy - Adams, William P.
  Raymoth - Hunter, Peyton

Ramy,
  Jemima - Hereford, John L.

Rea,
  Frances - Moore, Thomas
  Jemimah - Potter, Gidean R.
  Jinney - East, Joseph
  Lucinda - Rily, Daniel
  Lucy A. - Warthen, Walter G.
  Mary - Fulkeron, Frederick
  Mary - Soloman, Henry
  Mildred P. - Bouldin,
    Frederick H.
  Nancey - Cox, Larkin
  Nancy - Rea, Abner
  Polly - Leake, Garland
  Polly G. - Lindsey, John
  Prudence - Rea, George
  Rachel - Robertson, Joseph
  Sarah - Farris, Harrison
  Susanna - Phillips, Elisha

Reamey,
  Lettice - Hughes, Micajah
  Mary - Lanier, David

Reamy,
  Jemima - Hughes, Terry
  Polley - Rea, James

Redd,
  Anna - Starling, Thomas
  Anna E. S. - Booth, Moses G.
  Eliza. W. - Dillard, Peter H.
  Lucy D. - Wootton, John T.

Reed,
  Fanny - Cooksey, Edmund

Rentfroe,
  Sally - Staples, Jno.

Reynolds,
  Elizabeth - Jones, Peter

Rice,
  Sally - Casey, Thomas

Richards,
  Susa (?) - Jones, Robert

Richardson,
  Aggatha - Wyatt, Jno. P.
  Elenor - Wyatt, Craven
  Elinor - Burch, Gerrard
  Nancy - Burch, James

Riddle,
  Mary K. - Martin, William O.

Rives,
  Francis - Penn, Columbus

Roach,
  Nancy - Baley, James Baul
  Nancy - Jones, Bird

Roberts,
  Bethenia - Poston,
    Solomon
  Hannah - Martin, Joel
  Mary - Davis, Robert

Robertson,
  Eliza F. - Eggleton,
    Michael
  Lucinda - Bowles, Joseph
  Mary - Pratt, William J.
  Rachel - Land, Meshack
  Susan - Gravely, Edmond

Rogers,
  Eliza. - Ray, Reuben
  Nancy - Agee, Pleasant
  Patsy - Wells, Reuben

Rowland,
    Clarry - Nicholls, David
    Elizabeth - Chessure, Daniel
    Elizabeth - Heard, William
    Marion G. - Cheeley, William
    Mary - Beale, William, Jr.
    Sally M. - Hunter, Alexander

Royster,
    Martha C. - Thornton, James
    Patsey - Bouldin, Joseph, Jr.
    Susannah - Trahern, John

Ryan,
    Angellico - Lampkin, Lewis
    Mary - Richardson, John

Salmon,
    Abigail - Salmon, John
    Elizabeth - Williams, John
    Margaret - Dyer, Jefferson
    Martha - Holt, Harod
    Mary - Dyer, Joab
    Nancy - Dyer, David
    Nancy - Hensley, John
    Polly - Dyer, Joel
    Virginia - Rea, Iredell J.

Sampson,
    Mary - Williams, Bird
    Phoeba - McDaniel, John

Sams,
    Catharine - Doland, Charles

Sandford,
    Peggy - Crouch, Joseph

Sands,
    Sarah - Vaughan, Aris, Jr.

Scales,
    Ann - Beck, John
    Anna Hardin - Bouldin, Thomas C.
    Nancy - Pierce, Harrison
    Nancy H. - Fields, Nathaniel

Scrawyer,
    Mary A. - Wells, William

Seay,
    Mary - Irby, William

Self,
    Frances - Chesher, James

Shackelford,
    Jane - Woodall, James
    Mary - Pulliam, Drury

Shackleford,
    Elizabeth - Stults, Gabriel
    Lucy - Fortune, Joseph
    Harriet M. - Price, Duke
    Nancy - Dent, Benjamin
    Sally - Glass, James

Sheffield,
    Martha Ann - Booker, Edward

Shelton,
    Fanny - Abington, Wm. F.
    Judith - Scales, John P.
    Martha Ann - Taylor, George W.
    Mary - Penn, James
    Nancy - Hatcher, Archd., Jr.
    Ruth - Jones, Austin
    Sally - Mills, Aaron
    Susannah - Shelton, Alfred

Shewmate,
    Elizabeth - Pedigo, John L.

Shoemate,
    Agge - Smoot, George W.
    Polly - Litterell, Ire

Shumate,
    Delila - Montgomery, John
    Delilah - Smoote, John B.
    Mahaley - Haley, Benjamin
    Winefred - Graveley, John

Simes,
    Margaret - Woodall,
        Christopher T.

Simpson,
    Hester - Thomason, Joseph
    Prudence - Thomasson, James

Smith,
    Ann - Lawrence, James H.
    Betsey - Robertson, James
    Elizabeth - Lindsey, Henry
    Elizabeth - Martin, Isaac
    Elizabeth M. - Wood, Moses
    Martha - Merrick, Edward
    Mary Ann - Pedigo, Henry S.
    Nancy - Faris, Daniel
    Nancy - Lindsey, James

Smith (cont.),
Polly - Pearson, Peyton
Ruth - Taylor, German
Salley - Barksdale, Wm.
Salley - Gunn, Elisha
Sarah - Wells, Francis

Snell,
Ruth - Pratt, George

Southerland,
Pattsey - Simpson, Presley

Spencer,
America - Nicholas, Greenberry
Margaret - Dyer, George
Margaret - Wilks, Josiah
Mary - Clinton, Henry
Mary A. - Cheatham, Peter D.
Sally Ann - Allen, David M.

Stacy,
Caroline - Dakin, Preston
Salley - Stephens, William A.

Standifer,
Sally - Clack, John

Standifore,
Noami - Rentfro, Mark

Staples,
Ann W. - Sanders, William
Caroline - Finney, Joshua
Jane O. - Bassett, William N.
Martha - Hereford, Josiah
Martha Ann - Adkisson, John W.
Mary S. - Mathews, William
Polley - Waller, George, Jr.
Sally S. - Hairston, Hardin

Starling,
Elizabeth A. - Martin, George W.

Stephens,
Dorciss - Harriss, Moses
Leany - Hampton, Laban
Susannah - Wilson, Nathaniel
Susannah (or Hester Stevens) -
Hopper, William

Stewart,
Betsey - Mann, William (or Buck)

Steward (cont.),
Elizabeth - Warren, Jessee

Stockton,
Dolithear - Thompson,
William

Stokes,
Martha - Mitchell, William

Stone,
Ann - Hanes, Isaac N.
Dolly - Gravly, Willis
Elizabeth - Grogan, Richard
Elizabeth - Keenum, George
Mary Ann - Stone, Thos.
Milley - Walton, Elisha
Milly - Turner, George
Nancy - Grogan, Francis
Ruth - Walton, Pleasant
Sally Ann - Fagg, Charles
Wilmoth H. - Ellington,
James D.

Stovall,
Caroline - Staples, George

Stratton,
Elizabeth - Gilley, Joseph
Nancy - Gilley, Benjamin
Trifinia - Pratt, John

Stuart,
Ann A. - Brown, William

Stults,
Caty - Griggs, Michael
Elizabeth - Richardson, John
Joyce - Minter, Otheniel
Martha Jane - Taylor, James L.
Nancy - Minter, Silas
Nelly - Hicks, Thomas C.
Patsey - Williams, Abraham
Permelia - Gravly, Joseph K.
Sarah F. - Griggs, John G.

Stultz,
Delila - Eggleton, Nathaniel
Cassandra B. - Clark, Gideon
Lucinda D. - Atkins, John
Parthenia G. - Lyle,
Jefferson

Sturgeon,
    Enes - Rowland, John

Sumpter,
    Matilda E. - Tio, William

Suttenfield,
    Alice - Kington, Joseph

Suttonfield,
    Martha - Wray, Samuel P.

Swanson,
    Frances - Edmundson, Humphrey

Tabb,
    Keziah - Going, Simeon

Tarry,
    Sarah - Hunt, James

Taylor,
    Adeline Jane - Shelton, James
    Charity - May, John
    Eliza - Glass, Armistead W.
    Eliza. - Mabe, William
    Elizabeth - Stults, Adam
    Lucy A. - Martin, Richard
    Martha - Pitman, James
    Mary - Gouldin, Wesley
    Mary - Martin, Hudson
    Mary E. - Joice, Alexander
    Mary H. - Davis, Patrick H.
    Molly - Hawkins, Benjamin
    Nancy G. - Suttenfield, James M.
    Polley - Cooper, Elisha
    Sarah E. - Boaz, Stephen M.
    Susannah - Vawter, Chadwell
    Zaporah - Bishop, James
    Zerichia - McDaniel, Joel

Teel,
    Teresse - Jarrett, Robert

Terrell,
    Martha - Royster, Banister

Thacker,
    Eliza. - Webb (?), Robert
    Silvey - Byrd, Mason

Thomas,
    Caroline - Wyatt, Harrison
    Julia C. - Gravely, Benjamin F.

Thomas (cont.),
    Lubinda - Wyatt, Wesley S.
    Martha A. W. - Hamlett,
      William J.
    Susan - Wilmoth, William

Thomason,
    Elizabeth - Barrow, Jessee
    Joyce - Haley, Tavner
    Lucy - Thomason, John
    Polley - Simpson, Rodham
    Sarah - Fleeman, Thomas
    Winney - Harvil, Marcus

Thomasson,
    Fanny - Payne, John L.
    Jane - Nunn, Riley
    Mary - Hailey, Edward
    Nancy - Tyree, John

Thommasson,
    Jane - Smith, Brice

Thompson,
    Roxy A. - Mitchell, Jesse T.

Thornton,
    Patsey - Mageehee, Angus

Thurston,
    Elizabeth - East, William

Tinsley,
    Mary Ann - Millner, Thomas F.
    Sarah Ann - Millener,
      Marguis D. L.

Toler,
    Ann C. - Dearin, James

Toney,
    Lucy B. - Burton, Robert P.

Toombs,
    Susanna - Corsey, Charles

Travis,
    Frances Margaret - Wells,
      James M.

Trent,
    America - Lester, Jesse
    Kitty B. - Wootton,
      William H.
    Lucinda - Stanley, Swinfield

Trent (cont.),
  Polina D. - Wootton, Thomas J.
  Rachel W. - Price, Duke

Trotter,
  Amanda - Perkins, James H.

Turner,
  Addelpa - Turner, Shores
  Ann - Thomas, Joseph
  Elizabeth - Sumpter, George
  Jane - Phifer, James
  Mary Jane - Draper, John W.
  Nancy B. - Thomasson, William
  Polly - Pelfrey, James

Tyson,
  Mary Amelia - ----, Simeon C.

Vaughan,
  Caty - Burchett, Benjamin
  Nancy - Duncan, Archibald

Vintson,
  Leah - Elkins, James

Wade,
  Elizabeth - Hays, William, Jr.
  Judith - Mays, Jessee
  Polley - Smith, William
  Rachel - Gray, William
  Salley - Williams, Ozborne
  Sally - Allen, Joseph

Walker,
  Elizabeth - Anderson, John
  Elizabeth R. - Philpott, John J.

Waller,
  Eliza - Waller, George, Jr.
  Eliza. - King, John
  Malinda - Bassett, Burwell
  Martha M. - Pritchett, Henry
  Martha S. - Brewer, William P.
  Penelope C. - McCraw, Geo.
  Polley - King, George
  Sally H. - Williams, Elam
  Sarah - Hanby, William
  Sarah - Watson, Henry D.
  Sarah J. - Reamy, Peter R.
  Sarah Matilda - Edwards, Henry

Warham,
  Martha - Taylor, James

Warren,
  Armin - Parsley, James
  Eveland - Marshall, William
  Fanny - Garner, Thomas
  Jeane - Maupin, George

Wash,
  Elizabeth - Rowland, John,Jr.
  Salley - Nunn, Waters

Watkins,
  Caroline - Samms, Elijah
  Elizabeth P. - Southall,
    William P.
  Magdalene D. - Shelton, Peter
  Martha - Hubbard, Moses

Watson,
  Jane - Garrett, William
  Jean - Vaughan, William
  Lucy - Cox, Thomas
  Rhoda V. - Wilson,
    Jackson D. M.
  Winney - Bell, George W.

Watts,
  Nancy - Sutton, Charles

Weatherford,
  Mary - Bryant, Eli

Weaver,
  Nancy B. - Bouldin, William
  Polly - Burgess, John
  Rachel B. - Travis, Abner
  Susannah - Marshall, James D.

Webb,
  Fanny - Dooley, Thomas
  Lucy - Dooley, Thomas
  Salley - East, William

Wells,
  Ann R. - Bouldin, Obediah C.
  Catharine T. - Ivy, Nelson
  Eliza - Ayers, Murphey
  Elizabeth E. - Ivil, John
  Matilda - Wells, John
  Patey - Agee, Lewis

Wells (cont.),
  Patience - Pratt, Felix
  Susannah - Ivy, John W.

West,
  Elizabeth - Farris, Coleman
  Frances - Marshall, Elias
  Mary - Rea, Joseph

Whirly,
  Martha A. - May, Sanford

Wiatt,
  Susannah - Kimbrough, William

Williams,
  Elizabeth - Conway, John
  Elizabeth - Taylor, James
  Harriet M. - Pace, Jerman W.
  Patsey - Davis, John
  Polley - Atkinson, Jessee

Williamson,
  Ann - Woody, Allen

Wills,
  Dessa - McBride, Jacob
  Frances - Griggs, George
  Judith - Gravely, Jabez

Willson,
  Eliza J. - Nunnally, Thos. W.

Wilson,
  Delila - King, James
  Elly - Wilson, Thomas
  Jane - Gilley, James M.
  Jane - Harris, Daniel
  Lavina - Gilley, George
  Liddy - Land, William
  Lydia - Bailey, John
  Mary - Gilley, Benjm.
  Mary - Goodman, William
  Molley - Dunn, Hezekiah
  Patsey - Kannon, James
  Permelia - Robertson, Joseph
  Pheba - Turner, William
  Ruth - Land, Shadrick
  Salenia Ann - Crouch, Woodson
  Venia (?) - Daniel, John

Wingfield,
  Martha Ann - Gravely, Peyton

Witt,
  Lindy - Phifer, Joseph
  Tabitha - Dillen, William, Jr.

Witty,
  Elizabeth - Dillen,
   Benjamin, Jr.

Woodall,
  Nancy - Woodall, Jessee

Woodleif,
  Jeaney - Rea, John

Woods,
  Isbell - Dickerson, John

Worrell,
  Sarah - Taylor, William

Wray,
  Biddy - Bryant, Banister

Wyatt,
  Chancy - Wyatt, Vincent
  Chaney - Eggleton, Joseph
  Lettice - Davis, George
  Nancy - Lovell, Daniel

MINISTERS' RETURNS

May - 1849	Abington, William M., and Mary J. Philpot. R. P. Bibb, Minister.
Returns dated Aug. 24, 1790	Acuff, John, and Nan Watson. Carter Tarrant, Minister.
Returns dated July 24, 1783	Adams, Absalom, and Sarah Sumpter. William Lovell, Minister.
Jan. 22, 1789	Addams, Edward, and Betsey Taylor. Joseph Anthony, Minister.
Returns dated May 27, 1784	Adkins, David, and Judith ----. Publication. William Lovell, Minister.
Returns dated Aug, 24, 1790	Agee, Adly, and Joice Maston. Carter Tarrant, Minister.
Sept. 10, 1806	Agee, William, and Elizabeth Pursell. James Patterson, Minister.
Dec. 9, 1840	Aistrop, John, and Sarah Gilbert.
Return dated 1835	Allen, David, and Sally Ann Spencer, John C. Traylor.
Oct. 1, 1807	Allen, Joseph, and Sally Wade. Mannin Hill, Minister.
Sept. 6, 1807	Allen, Pines, and Charlotte Bayley. James Patterson, Minister.
--- - 1821	Allen, Pines, and Nancy Hughes. J. C. Traylor, Minister.
--- - ----	Allen, William, and Patsy Jones. David Nowlin, Minister.
Sept. 17, 1783	Allen, Saml., and Sarah Prater. John Newman, Minister.
Sept. 15, 1831	Alleson, Robert, and Mary L. Christian. Maning Hill, Minister.
Mar. 12, 1807	Allexander, Joseph, and Nancy Bouldin. James Patterson, Minister.
Return for 1797	Anderson, John, and Elizabeth Walker. John King, Minister.
June 4, 1845	Anderson, Seward G., and Nancy Hopper. Arthur W. Eanes, Minister.

Feb. 15, 1807	Armstead, Samuel, and Sally Martin. James Patterson, Minister.
May 14, 1810	Armstead, Francis, and Sally Hale. James Patterson, Minister.
May 12, 1829	Armstrong, Theophilous, and Milly Burgess. Othniel Minter, Minister.
Feb. 24, 1825	Arnold, James, and Julia Barrow. Arnold Walker, Minister.
Feb. 9, 1813	Arther, David, and Jincy Grigg. William Davis, Minister.
Mar. - 1842	Arthur, Joseph, and Rachel Feazle. A. Walker, Minister.
May 22, 1834	Artis, Jeff ("free man of colour"), and Ann Cousins ("free woman of colour"). Othniel Minter, Minister.
Return dated 1835	Ashby, Shelton, and Polly Pleasted. John C. Traylor, Minister.
Return dated 1835	Astrop, Jessee, and Louisa Morris. John C. Traylor, Minister.
May 13, 1816	Athey, Benjamin, and Jane Cheatham. John C. Taylor, Minister.
Feb. 10, 1817	Athy, Benjamin, and Jane Cheatham. John C. Taylor, Minister.
Undated	Atkinson, Amos A., and ----- -----.
Dec. 27, 1807	Atkinson, Jessee, and Polly Williams, Mannin Hill, Minister.
Feb. 5, 1829	Austin, Garland A., and Elizabeth I. Hawkins. Richard B. Beck, Minister.
Dec. 12, 1826	Austin, Danl., and Mary A. Hankins. Orson Martin, Minister.
July 14, 1835	Austin, Jefferson, and Ann S. Hankins. Orson Martin, Minister.
Jan 28, 1825	Austin, John, and (Oney) Allen. Orson Martin, Minister.
Undated	Ayres, Murphy, and Eliza Wells. Silas Minter, Minister.

--- - ---	Bailey, James, and Elizabeth Holland. William Lovell, Minister.
Aug. 9, 1795	Bailey, James Ball, and Nancy Roach. Clement Nance, Minister.
Jan. 15, 1783	Bailey, Samuel, and Lamet (?) Huff. Nathan Hall, Minister.
Dec. 27, 1831	Baker, George, and Elizabeth Dillian. Silas Minter, Minister.
Jan. 4, 1813	Baker, Jeremiah, and Milly Pace. Lewis Foster, Minister.
May 10, 1836	Barding, John M., and Elizabeth J. Martin. Arthur W. Eanes, Minister.
Mar. 7, 1836	Barker, Burrel, and Jane McDaniel. William Davis, Minister.
May 2, 1839	Barker, Gwilliams, and Sarah Barker. Arthur W. Eanes, Minister.
Oct. 11, 1825	Barker, James, and Elizabeth Goodman. Arnold Walker, Minister
Jan. 2, 1833	Barnet, Thomas, and Martha Casey. William Davis, Minister.
Return dated 1835	Barrow, Benjamin, and Susan Watkins. John C. Traylor, Minister.
Oct. - 1839	Barrow, William M., and Elizabeth J. King. Arnold Walker, Minister.
Sept. 19, 1785	Barton, Wm., and Stephne Russel. Joseph Anthony, Minister.
Return dated Nov. 9, 1818	Bassett, Burwell, and Martha Bassett. John C. Traylor, Minister.
Oct. 26, 1841	Bassett, Burwell, and Malinda Waller. Wm. M. Schoolfield, Minister.
Apr. 28, 1829	Bassett, William, and Jane O. Staples. Maning Hill, Minister.
Apr. 13, 1819	Bateman, Azel, and Levinia Gilly. Othniel Minter, Minister.
Aug. 20, 1846	Bateman, George, and Mary Rebecca Grant. Arthur W. Eanes, Minister.
Return dated June 25, 1844	Bateman, John, and Elizabeth J. Cahall. Joseph H. Evans, Minister.

Dec. 9, 1847 — Beheler, William, and Frances Wingfield.
John R. Martin, Minister.

Apr. 1, 1841 — Bell, James N., and Milly Minter. Arthur W. Eanes,
Minister.

Aug. 3, 1788 — Billing, Isaack, and Susanah Jackson. Joseph Anthony,
Minister.

Dec. 1, 1827 — Birch, John, and Lucy Perkinson. Orson Martin,
Minister.

Oct. - 1837 — Bird, Lewis, and Frances Draper. Arnold Walker,
Minister.

Jan. 21, 1813 — Bird, Mason, and Silvy Thacker. Lewis Foster,
Minister.

Apr. 5, 1829 — Bishop, James, and Zaporah Taylor. William Davis,
Minister.

Feb. 16, 1841 — Bishop, William, and Sarah Carter. Joseph H. Eanes,
Minister.

Jan. 6, 1846 — Boaz, Stephen M., and Sarah E. Taylor. John
Robertson, Minister.

Jan. 7, 1830 — Bocock, Drury, and Sally Dorson. Othniel Minter,
Minister.

Undated — Bohannon, Henry, and Mary Matlock. By Publication.
Wm. Lovell, Minister.

Dec. 20, 1831 — Booker, Edward, and Martha Ann Sheffield.
Silas Minter, Minister.

June 2, 1807 — Bouldin, Joseph, Jr., and Patsy C. Royster.
James Patterson, Minister.

Return dated — Bouldin, Richard, and Sally East. John C. Taylor,
Jan. 23, 1818 — Minister.

Dec. - 1842 — Bowles, John M., and Mary Edwards. A. Walker,
Minister.

May - 1846 — Bowles, Joseph, and Lucinda Roberson. A. Walker,
Minister.

Jan. - 1839 — Bowles, Lewis, and Frances Nunn. Arnold Walker,
Minister.

Oct. 11, 1783 — Bowman, Robert, and Mary Peck. John Newman,
Minister.

Nov. 19, 1785 — Bradbarry, Lewis, and Sarah East. Joseph Anthony,
Minister.

Apr. 28, 1830   Bradberry, Mark, and Manuroy Dawson. Othniel
                 Minter, Minister.

Nov. 21, 1786   Bradberry, Richard, and Vitha Winney. Joseph
                 Anthony, Minister.

Sept. 10, 1835   Bradberry, Richard, and Judith Dillen. Othniel Minter,
                 Minister.

Apr. - 1841   Bradbury, Peter, and Elizabeth B. Feazle.
                 A. Walker, Minister.

Returns dated   Bray, Ambrose, and Mary Crouch. Carter Tarrant,
Aug. 24, 1790   Minister.

Returns dated   Bray, John, and Sarah Johnston. Othneil Minter,
Nov 25, 1819   Minister.

Nov. 21, 1838   Bray, John, and Lucy Hankins. John D. Hankins,
                 Minister.

Oct. 14, 1839   Brewer, John, and Maria Bottoms. John D. Hankins,
                 Minister.

Feb. 3, 1825   Briant, Banister, and Biddy Rea. Arnold Walker,
                 Minister.

Undated   Brim, David, and Michy Pratt. Silas Minter, Minister.

Dec. 16, 1824   Brim, Nicholas, and Elizabeth Hill. John Washburn,
                 Minister.

July 11, 1783   Briscoe, John, and Darkus Medcalf. By Publication.
                 John Newman, Minister.

Sept. 30, 1801   Brown, Starling, and Susanna Clark. Robert
                 Stockton, Minister.

Feb. 1, 1849   Brown, William, and Ann A. Stewart. Wm. M.
                 Schoolfield, Minister.

Oct. 28, 1839   Bryant, Elisha, and Lucy Hundley. Othniel Minter,
                 Minister.

Mar. 16, 1845   Bryant, James, and Martha Harger. Wellington E.
                 Webb, Minister.

June 16, 1783   Bryant, Thos., and Sarah Rogers. By Publication.
                 John Newman, Minister.

Oct. 15, 1829   Burch, Bazel, and Martha Laine. Orson Martin,
                 Minister.

Return dated   Burch, Gerrard, and Eleanor Richardson.
Feb. 11, 1839   Silas Minter, Minister.

Dec. 20, 1838	Burch, James, and Sintha Minter. Othniel Minter, Minister.
Nov. - 1832	Burges, Thomas, and Sarah Cox. Silas Minter, Minister.
--- - 1823	Burgess, Davis H., and Elizabeth Lanier. Arnold Walker, Minister.
Oct. 22, 1825	Burgess, John, and Polly Weaver. Othniel Minter, Minister.
Feb. 9, 1837	Burgess, John, and Matilda France. Othniel Minter, Minister.
Return for 1790 & 1791	Burnett, Bond, and Elizabeth Small. Robert Jones, Minister.
Aug. 2, 1792	Burnett, Moses, and Elizabeth Melvin. Joseph Anthony, Minister.
Sept. 3, 1802	Burrass, Jacob, and Ruth Dillion. Joseph Anthony, Minister.
Feb. 3, 1805	Burrus, George, and Elizabeth Taylor. Maning Hill, Minister.
Return dated Dec. 20, 1819	Burton, William, and Sary Clark. William Davis, Minister.
Nov. - 1842	Campbell, Caleb C., and Martha Jane Jarrett. A. Walker, Minister.
Jan 16, 179-?	Cannon (?), John, and Nancy Taylor. Andrew Hunter, Minister.
Nov. - 1842	Carper, Moses G., and Jane E. Jones. A. Walker, Minister.
Return dated Nov. 20, 178-?	Carrol, John, and Mary Hooker. Michael Dillingham, Minister.
Dec. 31, 1840	Carter, Cary, and Elizabeth Dillon.
May 17, 1846	Carter, Cary, and Elvira Duvall.
July - 1846	Carter, Fleming, and Martha Philpott. A. Walker, Minister.
Aug. 9, 1782	Carter, George, and Frances Richman. Nathan Hall, Minister.
Jan. 28, 1836	Carter, George, and Elizabeth Odel. William Davis, Minister.

July 27, 1847   Carter, Lawson H., and Virginia N. Meade.
                 Morrison Meade, father. James M. Wilson, Minister.

Jan. 22, 1827   Caton, Martin, and Nancy Pullom. William Davis,
                 Minister.

Jan. 11, 1783   Chadwick, Richard, and Esther Green. Nathan Hall,
                 Minister.

Mar. 16, 1787   Chandler, Thomas, and Charity Elliott. Joseph
                 Anthony, Minister.

Dec. - 1830   Chealey, William, and Marian G. Rowland.
                 Arnold Walker, Minister.

July 6, 1808   Cheatham, Edmond, and Francinia Bouldin. James
                 Patterson, Minister.

July 4, 1832   Cheatham, Henry E., and Mary S. Dillard.
                 Arnold Walker, Minister.

Jan. 17, 1844   Chesheir, James, and Frances Self. Othniel Minter,
                 Minister.

Return dated   Cheshier, Thomas, and Elizabeth A. Minter. Silas
1833   Minter, Minister.

July 19, 1837   Chessiere, Coleman, and Mary Land. Othniel Minter,
                 Minister.

Dec. 20, 1838   Chessure, Daniel, and Elizabeth Rowland.
                 Othniel Minter, Minister.

July 12, 1833   Choice, Gresham, and Casandra A. Jones. A. Walker,
                 Minister.

July 8, 1813   Clanton, Mackland, and Winny Oldham. William
                 Davis, Minister.

Jan. 12, 1842   Clanton, William F., and Virginia Pulliam.
                 Arthur W. Eanes, Minister.

Oct. 25, 1838   Clark, Gideon, and Cassandra Stults. Othniel Minter,
                 Minister.

Sept. 25, 1820   Clark, Isaac, and Susanna Gravely. Richard B. Beck,
                 Minister.

Nov. 25, 1833   Clark, Isack, and Elizabeth Haley. Nathan Anderson,
                 Minister.

Feb. 10, 1817   Clark, James, and Mourning Martin. John C. Taylor,
                 Minister.

Return dated   Clark, John, and Jane Clark. Joseph H. Evans,
June 25, 1844   Minister.

Dec. 28, 1820   Clark, Thomas, and Sally Carver. Richard B. Beck,
                 Minister.

Feb. 10, 1817   Clark, William, and M. Redd.   John C. Taylor, Minister.

Mar. 30, 1826   Clarke, William, and Cassandra Marshall.   Arnold Walker, Minister.

May 22, 1787   Clerk, David, and Elizabeth Stovall.   Joseph Anthony, Minister.

July 22, 1828   Clinkscales, James, and Jennette Dillard.   Othneil Minter, Minister.

Jan. - 1844   Clowers, George W., and Susan Davis.   Arnold Walker, Minister.

Mar. 16, 1826   Cobbs, Nelson, and Mary Gilley.   Arnold Walker, Minister.

Return dated 1833   Cobbs, John, and Margaret Waller.   Silas Minter, Minister.

Jan. 11, 1827   Cobler, John, and Sally Boulden.   Arnold Walker, Minister.

1783   Coger, Henry, and Mary King.   Wm. Lovell, Minister.

Mar. 30, 1808   Cole, Samuel, and Kitty Miller.   James Patterson, Minister.

Nov. - 1836   Coleman, James, and Caleneice Feazle.   Arnold Walker, Minister.

Dec. - 1848   Coleman, James, and Mary Ann Davis.   A. Walker, Minister.

1786   Colliar, Charles, and Lydia Preston.   William Lovell, Minister.

Sept. 1, 1785   Cook, Jesse, and Elizabeth Bohannon.   Robert Jones, Minister.

Oct. 8, 1828   Cook, Robert, and Susan Martin.   Arnold Walker, Minister.

Oct. 29, 1830   Cooper, Alexander, and Mary Nunn.   Arnold Walker, Minister.

Sept. - 1837   Cooper, Greenville, and Sally T. Allick.   Arnold Walker, Minister.

June 15, 1828   Cooper, Hubert, and Sally L. King.   Othniel Minter, Minister.

Dec. 19, 1839   Covington, John, and Sarah Pulliam.   Othniel Minter, Minister.

May 14, 1829   Cox, John, and Elizabeth Cox.   William Davis, Minister.

Aug. 21, 1828   Cox, Peter C., and Maryan Harris.   William Davis, Minister.

Nov. 3, 1846   Craghead, Thomas L., and Lucinda T. Baker.
Wm. M. Schoolfield, Minister.

--- - 1797   Craig, Thomas, and Polly Davis. John King, Minister.

Dec. 9, 1841   Craig, William, and Sally Oakley. Wm. M.
Schoolfield, Minister.

Return dated   Crane, Aaron, and Jean Harden. Michael Dillingham,
Nov. 20, 178-?   Minister.

May 13, 1841   Creasy, Henry, and Nancy Barker. Arthur W. Eanes,
Minister.

Nov. 2, 1836   Creasy, James, and Virginia Norman. Othniel Minter,
Minister.

Mar. 1, 1810   Creasy, Joseph, and Delilah Jones. James Patterson,
Minister.

July 1, 1809   Creasy, Thomas, and Nancy Davis. James Patterson,
Minister.

Dec. 20, 1821   Creay, Robert, and Polly Buck. William Davis, Minister.

Apr. - 1831   Crews, Gideon, and Eliza C. Bouldin. Arnold Walker,
Minister.

Aug. 18, 1830   Crews, Samuel, and Marial Hatcher. Maning Hill,
Minister.

Nov. 23, 1785   Crouch, John, and Elizabeth Bradberry. Joseph
Anthony, Minister.

Return dated   Crouch, Woodson, and Salina Ann Wilson.
Nov. 9, 1847   Joseph H. Eanes, Minister.

--- - 1786   Crowley, James, and Mary McClain. William Lovell,
Minister.

Feb. 22, 1810   Crunk, John, and Elizabeth Scales. William Davis,
Minister.

--- - ----   Cummins, Joseph, and Rosanna Medley. William
Lovell, Minister.

Sept. 13, 1787   Cunningham, William, and Frankey Purtle. Joseph
Anthony, Minister.

Dec. 28, 1837   Curry, William, and Harriet Pulliam. Othniel Minter,
Minister.

Feb. 18, 1834   Dandridge, Charles F., and Sally B. Winston.
Nathan Anderson, Minister.

Return dated   Darnall, John, and Mary Dyer. Silas Minter, Minister.
1835

June 16, 1783	Davidson, Richardson, and Ann Ward. By Publication. John Newman, Minister.
Jan. - 1838	Davis, Brice, and Nancy Lane. Arnold Walker, Minister.
Dec. 1, 1836	Davis, Coleman, and Nancy Cheshier. Othniel Minter, Minister.
Sept. 10, 1829	Davis, Israel, and Rachel Gilly. Richard B. Beck, Minister.
Returns dated Aug. 24, 1790	Davis, John, and Elizabeth Pedigo. Carter Tarrant, Minister.
Sept. 14, 1809	Davis, John, and Patsey Williams. James Patterson, Minister.
Apr. - 1848	Davis, Laban J., and Letitia Ann Pedigo. A. Walker, Minister.
Nov. 4, 1806	Davis, Robert, and Joanna Hewlett. James Patterson, Minister.
Mar. - 1808	Davis, Robert, and Mary Roberts. James Patterson, Minister.
Nov. - 1839	Davis, Thomas B., and Martha Coleman. Arnold Walker, Minister.
May 24, 1827	Dawson, John, and Elizabeth Peddigo. Othniel Minter, Minister.
Oct. 8, 1829	Delozier, Perin, and Francinia Minter. Richard B. Beck, Minister.
Aug. - 1821	Deshazo, George R., and Susannah Cahill. Othneil Minter, Minister.
Apr. 13, 1828	Deshazo, Richard, and Elizabeth Allen. Orson Martin, Minister.
May 11, 1847	Dickenson, William T., and Nancy Gravely. John Rich, Minister.
May 2, 1827	Dier, Joel, and Isbel Barker. William Davis, Minister.
Jan. 21, 1845	Dillard, Dr. Peter F., and Elizabeth P. Hairston. Wellington E. Webb, Minister.
June 3, 1818	Dillard, Peter H., and Elizabeth W. Read. Maning Hill, Minister.
Jan. 27, 1803	Dillard, George, and Patsey Hill. Joseph Anthony, Minister.
Feb. - 1843	Dillard, Overton R., and Salley Martin. Arnold Walker, Minister.

Sept. 19, 1825 Dillen, William, and Elizabeth Nunn. John C. Traylor, Minister.

Nov. 19, 1829 Dillen, William, and Susan Lanier. Oth. Minter, Minister.

Mar. 1, 1787 Dillian, John, and Sarah Whitton. Joseph Anthony, Minister.

Mar. 2, 1792 Dillingham, Lott, and Ann Dillingham. Joseph Anothy, Minister.

Feb. 21, 1839 Dillion, Elison, and Delila Carter. Othniel Minter, Minister.

Dec. 20, 1792 Dillion, Wm., and Tabitha Witt. Joseph Anthony, Minister.

June 30, 1783 Dillion, William, and Martha Dillion. By License. John Newman, Minister.

Sept. - 1824 Dillon, Jefferson, and Sarah Pace. Arnold Walker, Minister.

Aug. 4, 1846 Doland, Charles, and Catherine Sams.

Feb. 18, 1845 Donegan, Thomas E., and Elenor Gravely. Benja. M. Williams, Minister.

Aug. 11, 1831 Doss, John, and Catherine Philips. Maning Hill, Minister.

Feb. 21, 1837 Doyle, William M., and Elizabeth Minter. Othniel Minter, Minister.

Return dated Draper, Asa, and Sally Mitchell. James Patterson, Nov. 11, 1811 Minister.

Sept. - 1845 Draper, John W., and Mary Jane Turner. A. Walker, Minister.

Jan. 1, 1828 Draper, Thomas, and Nancy Davis. Othniel Minter, Minister.

Dec. 23, 1845 Draper, William F., and Mary Good. Jeremiah Burnett, Minister.

Dec. 27, 1843 Dunavant, James, and Rebecca Mills. Othniel Minter, Minister.

Oct. 16, 1785 Dunn, Gatewood, and Martha Swanson. Joseph Anthony, Minister.

Feb. 13, 1845 Dunn, James D., and Ann Lewis. Arthur W. Eanes, Minister.

Undated Durham, ----, and Nancy Vaughan.

Aug. 24, 1792	Durossett (?), Daniel, and Nancy Wheat. Joseph Anthony, Minister.
Mar. 9, 1816	Dyer, David, and Nancy Salmon. James Patterson, Minister.
Jan. 12, 1831	Dyer, Fountain, and Harriet Cheely. Silas Minter, Minister.
Nov. 3, 1825	Dyer, George, and Margaret Spencer. Othneil Minter, Minister.
Oct. 2, 1834	Dyer, George, and Nancy George. Othniel Minter, Minister.
Feb. 22, 1832	Dyer, James, and Julia Williamson. Othniel Minter, Minister.
Apr. 26, 1835	Dyer, James M., and Amanda M. C. Grigg. Othniel Minter, Minister.
Undated	Dyer, Jefferson, and Elizabeth Carter. Silas Minter, Minister.
Return dated Feb. 11, 1839	Dyer, Joab, and Nancy B. Harvey. Silas Minter, Minister.
Return dated Nov. 11, 1811	Dyer, Joel, and Polly Salmon. James Patterson, Minister.
Nov. - 1824	Dyer, Joel, and Mary Salmon. Arnold Walker, Minister.
Apr. 14, 1835	Dyer, Joseph, and Mary Haily. Othniel Minter, Minister.
Nov. 11, 1787	Eades, Abraham, and Mary Mullins. Joseph Anthony, Minister.
Return dated Nov. 9, 1847	Eanes, Blair H., and Catharine Nance. Joseph H. Eanes, Minister.
Aug. 7, 1782	Easley, Miller Woodson, and Mary Lyon. Nathan Hall, Minister.
Feb. 10, 1817	East, John, and Betsy Pane. John C. Taylor, Minister.
July 24, 1834	East, William, and Sarah Philpott. A. Walker, Minister.
Nov. - 1835	Easton, Daniel, and Tabitha W. Bradbury. Arnold Walker, Minister.
Sept. 24, 1823	Edwards, Brice (?), and Martha Barksdale. Orson Martin, Minister.
--- - 1823	Edwards, Chiles, and Nancy D. Hewlett. Arnold Walker, Minister.

Sept. - 1849   Edwards, James M., and Elizabeth A. Good.
                A. Walker, Minister.

Return dated   Edwards, John, and Jean Morris. William Lovell,
July 24, 1783   Minister.

Aug. - 1849   Edwards, Steven, and Elizabeth M. Dillion. A. Walker,
                Minister.

Aug. - 1840   Edwards, William R., and Jane Bowles. Arnold Walker,
                Minister.

Nov. - 1828   Egelton, Michael, and Eliza F. Robertson. Arnold Walker,
                Minister.

Sept. 6, 1826   Egelton, Thomas, and Docia Pace. Arnold Walker,
                Minister.

Mar. - 1850   Eggleton, Henry H., and Mary D. Winn. A. Walker,
                Minister.

June 26, 1834   Eggleton, Moses, and Martha Cheshier. Othniel Minter,
                Minister.

Return dated   Eggleton, Stephen, and Leanna Haley. Silas Minter,
1833   Minister.

Return dated   Egleton, George, and Nancy Bouldin. John C. Traylor,
Jan. 23, 1818   Minister.

Mar. 18, 1829   Egleton, Joseph, and Chaney Wyatt. Orson Martin, Minister.

Nov. - 1841   Egleton, Nathaniel, and Delia Stultz. A. Walker, Minister.

Dec. 24, 1783   Elkins, William, and Eliza. East. John Newman, Minister.

Sept. 25, 1844 Ellington, James D., and Wilmoth H. Stone. John Rich,
                Minister.

Return dated   Elston, James, and Zelpha Gunn. John C. Traylor,
Jan. 23, 1818   Minister.

Nov. 24, 1844   Faris, George W., and Adeline Bryant. Wm. M.
                Schoolfield, Minister.

Return dated   Farris, Harrison, and Sarah Rea. Maning Hill,
Nov. 16, 1819   Minister.

May - 1836   Feazle, Joab, and Jane Nunn. Arnold Walker, Minister.

June - 1792   (Ferrell)?, Thomas, and Judith Quarles. Joseph
                Anthony, Minister.

Jan. 27, 1788   Ferriss, Archarbald, and Frances Hix. Joseph Anthony, Minister.

Nov. 3, 1788   Ferriss, Josiah, and Polly Stovall. Joseph Anthony, Minister.

Jan. 12, 1792   Ferriss, Thomas, and Judith Qualls. Joseph Anthony, Minister.

Return dated Nov. 20, 178-?   Feuson, John, and Hannah Brunk. Michael Dillingham, Minister.

Return dated Nov. 16, 1819   Field, Nathaniel, and Nancy Hulet (Scales). William Davis, Minister.

Apr. 11, 1803   Fifer, Bradly, and Polly Hibbert. Joseph Anthony, Minister.

Aug. 16, 1808   Fifer, Joseph, and Lindy Witt. Lewis Foster, Minister.

Sept. 26, 1785   Finch, William, and Jean East. Joseph Anthony, Minister.

Feb. 16, 1832   Finney, John, and Frances King. Othniel Minter, Minister.

Feb. 20, 1849   Finney, Joshua, and Caroline Staples. Wm. M. Schoolfield, Minister.

Feb. 4, 1810   Fishback, William, and Permelia Johnston. James Patterson, Minister.

Dec. 6, 1849   Flanagan, Burwell, and Martha Odle. George W. McNeely, Minister.

Nov. 19, 1840   Flanegan, Beverly, and Nancy Odle. Arthur W. Eanes, Minister.

Apr. 13, 1809   Fleeman, John, and Eliza. Griffin. James Patterson, Minister.

Apr. 10, 1839   Fleeman, Hezekiah, and Eithy Carter. John D. Hankins, Minister.

Return dated Jan. 20, 1820   Fleeman, Thomas, and Sarah Thomason. Othneil Minter, Minister.

Apr. 13, 1819   Flemon, George, and Martha Perkinson. Othniel Minter, Minister.

Sept. 16, 1783   Fletcher, John, and Miriam Parr. John Newman, Minister.

Feb. 5, 1832   Flood, Washington, and Mary Jane Morris. Othniel Minter, Minister.

Oct. 9, 1828   Floyd, Benjamin, and Melinda Moore. Maning Hill, Minister.

Aug. 14, 1828 Floyd, William P., and Jane S. Mills. Maning Hill, Minister.

Dec. 5, 1791 Folas (?), Hugh, and Barbary Hunley. Joseph Anthony, Minister.

Aug. 7, 1849 Fontaine, Charles H., and Martha C. Nowlin. George W. Dame, Minister.

Return dated Fontaine, John, and Mary C. Reid. John C. Taylor, May 13, 1816 Minister.

Return dated Forbes, Augustine, and Nancy East. John C. Traylor, 1836 Minister.

Nov. 16, 1809 Foster, John, and Elizabeth Foster. James Patterson, Minister.

Feb. 16, 1809 Fortune, Joseph, and Lucy Shackleford. James Patterson, Minister.

Apr. 18, 1791 France, John, and Elizabeth Clark. Andrew Hunter, Minister.

Apr. 21, 1836 Francis, Matthew, and Mary Allen. William Davis, Minister.

Mar. 21, 1787 Franklin, Lewis, and Milly Stone. Joseph Anthony, Minister.

Return dated Franklin, William, and Martha Hunly. John C. Traylor, 1835 Minister.

Oct. 6, 1808 Frazer (?), Ellexander, and Polley Marady (?). Lewis Foster, Minister.

Feb. 16, 1832 Frazier, George W., and Sarah Dillon. Othniel Minter, Minister.

July 10, 1783 French, Joseph, and Judith Smith. By Publication. John Newman, Minister.

July 3, 1783 French, Wm., and Betsey Abbington. By Publication. John Newman, Minister.

Dec. 20, 1832 Fretwell, Charles, and Nancy Marshall. William Davis, Minister.

July 27, 1837 Fretwell, William, and Mary J. Norman. Arthur W. Eanes, Minister.

Oct. 30, 1845 Fry, Archilus, and Naney M. Lawrence.

May 20, 1824 Fulkerson, Frederick, and Mary Rea. Maning Hill, Minister.

Return for Garner, Obediah, and Hellen Nance. John King, Minister. 1797

Dec. 18, 1845	Garrot (Jarrot), John, and Susan E. Bradley, William Schoolfield, Minister.
Apr. 18, 1792	Garrott, Elimeleck, and Sally Vaughan. Joseph Anthony, Minister.
Return dated 1790	Gaskit, Enuck, and Hannah Carter. Jesse Rentfro, Minister.
Dec. 22, 1831	Gear, Reubin, and Casah Meredith. Othniel Minter, Minister.
Dec. 8, 1788	Gibson, John, and Hanner Fitzgerrell. Joseph Anthony, Minister.
July 6, 1788	Gibson, William, and Mary Shard. Joseph Anthony, Minister.
Feb. 21, 1831	Gilbert, Greensville, and ---- ------. Maning Hill, Minister.
Jan. 28, 1840	Gilley, Alfred, and Harriet Cayton. Othniel Minter, Minister.
Oct. 27, 1831	Gilley, Charles, and Elizabeth F. Mills. Arnold Walker, Minister.
Feb. 3, 1842	Gilley, Leftwich, and Mary Gilley.
Jan. 7, 1841	Gilley, Samuel, and Martha Cox.
Mar. 3, 1842	Glass, Armistead W., and Eliza Taylor, Arthur W. Eanes, Minister.
Nov. 30, 1821	Goldin, Andra, and Unity Bray. William Davis, Minister.
Aug. 1, 1830	Goode, Thomas, and Coley Barber. Othniel Minter, Minister.
Oct. 18, 1825	Goodman, David, and Agness Harris. Arnold Walker, Minister.
Feb. 9, 1832	Goodman, David, and Mariam Harris. Richard B. Beck, Minister.
Apr. 10, 1805	Goolsby, Charles, and Armine Anglin. Maning Hill, Minister.
Jan. 24, 1829	Gorthat, John, and Polly Purgusson. Orson Martin, Minister.
Mar. 7, 1782	Graveley, James, and Mary Harper. Peter Smith, Minister.
Nov. 5, 1832	Gravelley, Willis, and Ann M. Barrow. Othniel Minten, Minister.
Dec. - 1845	Gravely, Benjamin L., and Julia C. Thomas. A. Walker, Minister.

Nov. 12, 1825   Gravely, Edmund, and Susan Robertson. William Davis, Minister.

Feb. 16, 1826   Gravely, George, and Mary M. Hughes. Arnold Walker, Minister.

Return for 1797   Gravely, Jabez, and Judith Wells. John King, Minister.

Jan. 13, 1835   Gravely, Jabez L., and Martha L. Hankins. Orson Martin, Minister.

Jan. 1, 1824   Gravely, John, and Frances Marshall. John C. Traylor, Minister.

Jan. 24, 1826   Gravely, John, and Winefred Shumate. Arnold Walker, Minister.

Nov. - 1846   Gravely, Peyton, and Martha Ann Wingfield. John R. Martin, Minister.

Oct. - 1847   Gravely, Peyton, and Matilda F. Thomas. A. Walker, Minister.

Feb. 9, 1831   Gravely, William, and Lidia Clark. Richard B. Beck, Minister.

Dec. 23, 1824   Gravely, Willis, and Dolly Stone. Arnold Walker, Minister.

Dec. 29, 1821   Gravley, Lewis, and Martha Dyer. Othneil Minter, Minister.

Mar. 27, 1805   Gray, William, and Rachel Wade. Maning Hill, Minister.

Feb. 28, 1811   Greenlee, David, and Martha Hunter. Lewis Foster, Minister.

Jan. 1, 1807   Greenlee, Ephram M., and Sally Howard. Lewis Foster, Minister.

Apr. 4, 1837   Gregory, Fleming, and Nancy W. Harris. Othniel Minter, Minister.

Jan. 18, 1832   Gregory, John, and Susannah King. Othniel Minter, Minister.

Mar 19, 1839   Gregory, William, and Lucy Dillion. Othniel Minter, Minister.

Dec. 24, 1843   Gregory, William, and Eliza Jones. Othniel Minter, Minister.

Aug. 3, 1782   Griffith, William, and Susanah Jones. Nathan Hall, Minister.

Nov. - 1836   Griggs, Ira, and Sally King. Arnold Walker, Minister.

Aug. 2, 1792	Griggs, John, and Phebe Auns (?). Joseph Anthony, Minister.
Nov. 19, 1820	Griggs, Michael, and Sally Peddigo. Othneil Minter, Minister.
Dec. - 1838	Griggs, Peter F., and Dorritha Clanton. Arnold Walker, Minister.
Return dated Feb. 11, 1839	Griggs, Wesley, and Susan W. King. Silas Minter, Minister.
Sept. 3, 1826	Grogan, Bartholemew, and Patsy Stone. Arnold Walker, Minister.
Apr. 12, 1821	Grogan, Francis, and Nancy Stone. Maning Hill, Minister.
Mar. 7, 1847	Grogan, John W., and Martha J. Phariss. Othneil Minter, Minister.
Jan. 20, 1825	Grogan, Richard, and Elizabeth Stone. Arnold Walker, Minister.
Mar. 4, 1832	Grogin, Francis, and Elizabeth Hopper. William Davis, Minister.
Aug. 11, 1813	Guset, Cabin, and Polly Phifer. Lewis Foster, Minister.
Apr. 19, 1827	Gyer, Joseph, and Susan Dillion. Othniel Minter, Minister.
Return dated Aug. 30, 1795	Hailey, John, and Lucy Ryon. John King, Minister.
Dec. 26, 1792	Hailey, Wm., and Nancy Jackson. Joseph Anthony, Minister.
July - 1837	Hairston, George S., and Matilda M. Martin. Arnold Walker, Minister.
June 2, 1808	Hairston, Hardin, and Sally S. Staples. Mannin Hill, Minister.
Mar. 4, 1783	Hales, John, and Edee East. Nathan Hall, Minister.
July 10, 1833	Haley, Benjamin, and Mahely Shumate. Nathan Anderson, Minister.
Feb. 20, 1834	Haley, John W., and Mary Philpott. A. Walker, Minister.
Dec. 11, 1834	Haley, Thomas J., and Nancy Lester. Arnold Walker, Minister.
May - 1850	Haley, William S., and Eliza A. Lester. A. Walker, Minister.

Dec. 24, 1824 Hall, John, and Temperance Hawkins. Orson Martin, Minister.

Oct. 14, 1835 Hamlett, William J., and Martha A. Thomas. Arnold Walker, Minister.

July 15, 1789 Hamor, Daniel, and Mary Martain. Joseph Anthony, Minister.

Jan. - 1849 Hanby, Hiram B., and Martha Edwards. A. Walker, Minister

Apr. 16, 1787 Hanner, William, and Lucy Penn. Joseph Anthony, Minister.

July 6, 1783 Harbour, David, and Easter Crunk. By Publication. John Newman, Minister.

May 24, 1827 Hardy, John, and Sarah Peddigo. Othniel Minter, Minister.

Apr. 6, 1830 Hardy, Joseph, and Nancy Pace. Othniel Minter, Minister.

May 11, 1837 Harfield, David J., and Elizabeth J. Devin. Arthur W. Eanes, Minister.

Jan. 1, 1821 Haris, Filler, and Sally Bateman. William Davis, Minister.

Return for 1790 & 1791 Harper, Jessee, and Hannah Ratliff. Robert Jones, Minister.

July 12, 1827 Harris, Daniel, and Jane Wilson. Othniel Minter, Minister.

July 27, 1848 Harris, George, and Milly Harris, dau. of Lizza Harris. James M. Wilson, Minister, Presbyterian.

Jan. 26, 1826 Harris, James, and Lucy Jones. William Davis, Minister.

Returns show Oct. 1, 1781 to Mar. 20, 1782 Harris, Jonathan, and Ann Heard. Michael Dillingham, Minister.

--- - 1821 Harris, Joseph, and Elizabeth Hill. J. C. Traylor, Minister.

Apr. 10, 1782 Harris, William, and Lidde Renfro. Nathan Hall, Minister.

Dec. 20, 1832 Harriss, Thomas E., and Ann Pulliem. Othniel Minter, Minister.

Dec. 17, 1807 Harvel, Marcus, and Winny Thomason. James Patterson, Minister.

Return dated 1835	Harvell, Merrit, and Tabitha Minter. Silas Minter, Minister.
Jan. 23, 1825	Harvey, Lewis, and Ann Cobbs. Arnold Walker, Minister.
Dec. 19, 1849	Harvill, George A., and Mary A. Barker. Hezekiah Smith, Minister.
Oct. 26, 1807	Hatcher, Archibald, and Nancy Shelton. Mannin Hill, Minister.
Nov. 26, 1843	Hay, William P., and Susan L. Mathews. William Schoolfield, Minister.
Undated	Hays, William, and Elizabeth Lemons. By Publication. Jesse Rentfro, Minister.
July 7, 1791	Heath, William, and Sally Belt Watson. Andrew Hunter, Minister.
Nov. 29, 1804	Hemming, William, and Delilah McKensey. Maning Hill, Minister.
Oct. 27, 1845	Hensley, William, and Frances Ann Bocock. Benja. M. Williams, Minister.
Return dated Jan. 23, 1818	Hereford, John, and Jemima Rayney. John C. Traylor, Minister.
Jan. 1, 1824	Hereford, Josiah, and Martha Staples. John C. Traylor, Minister.
Return dated Jan. 23, 1818	Hereford, William, and Ann Dandridge. John C. Traylor, Minister.
Nov. 23, 1825	Hester, Wiley, and Margaret Mullins. John Turner, Minister.
Jan. 7, 1796	Hewlett, William, and Elizabeth Burgess. Clement Nance, Minister.
Sept. 23, 1787	Hickman, Edwin, and Elizabeth Pryar. Joseph Anthony, Minister.
June 29, 1825	Hickman, William H., and Elizabeth Ann Christian. Maning Hill, Minister.
Return dated Dec. 26, 1819	Hicks, Thomas C., and Nelly Stults. Othneil Minter, Minister.
--- - 1783	Hill, John, and Sarah Hollensworth. Wm. Lovell, Minister.
Feb. 10, 1817	Hill, John W., and Judith Hill. John C. Taylor, Minister.

Dec. 10, 1826   Hill, Maning, and Elizabeth L. Gunnell. Arnold
Walker, Minister.

Feb. 25, 1836   Hill, Robert S., and Mary Lanier. Othniel Minter,
Minister.

Nov. 19, 1840   Hill, William M., and Mary Catherine Bassett. Wm. M.
Schoolfield, Minister.

--- - 1786   Hilton, Edward, and Sarah Woody. William Lovell, Minister.

--- - 1786   Hilton, John, and Martha Mayberry. William Lovell,
Minister.

Dec. 23, 1847   Hodges, Alexander, and Frances Hatcher. John R. Martin,
Minister.

Return dated   Hodges, John, and Fidiles Clark. Silas Minter, Minister.
Feb. 11, 1839

Oct. 1, 1829   Hodges, Obediah, and Elizabeth Fleeman. Orson Martin,
Minister.

Sept. 12, 1844   Holland, William, and Sarah W. Norman. Arthur W.
Eanes, Minister.

Dec. 14, 1820   Hollandsworth, Brice, and Ann Garrett Philpott.
Othneil Minter, Minister.

Jan. 1, 1824   Hollandsworth, Thomas, and Mary Nunn. John C. Traylor,
Minister.

Aug. 18, 1786   Hollingsworth, Isaak, and Elizabeth Newman. Joseph
Anthony, Minister.

Apr. - 1836   Holloway, John H., and Martha Hibberts. Arnold
Walker, Minister.

Undated   Holloway, William, and Caty Poteet. William Lovell,
Minister.

June 20, 1789   Holt, John, and Polly Jones. Joseph Anthony, Minister.

Dec. 10, 1822   Holt, Paskel, and Rachel Jones. William Davis, Minister.

Return dated   Homes, Benjamin, and Elizabeth Thomas. Wm. Lovell,
1783   Minister.

Nov. 22, 1842   Hopper, Allen, and Eliza Bassett. Wm. M. Schoolfield,
Minister.

July 19, 1821   Hopper, James, and Elizabeth Base. William Davis,
Minister.

Dec. 28, 1847   Hopper, James H., and Judith H. Hatcher, Daniel G.
Taylor, Minister.

Aug. 6, 1822   Hopper, John, and Jane Lemon. William Davis, Minister.

Feb. 17, 1847   Hopper, William, and Elizabeth Plumer. Arthur W. Eanes, Minister.

Returns dated Aug. 24, 1790   Howard, James, and Rachel Stockton. Carter Tarrant, Minister.

Sept. 18, 1783   Howell, Joseph, and Lucy Smith. John Newman, Minister.

Aug. 12, 1835   Huberd, Moses, and Martha Watkins. Orson Martin, Minister.

Dec. 21, 1847   Hudnall, Charles, and Sophia Suttenfield. Daniel G. Taylor, Minister.

Return dated Nov. 11, 1819   Hudson, Daniel, and Sophia Clinkscales. Maning Hill, Minister.

Nov. 30, 1847   Huff, Bird, and Emily Lavinder. John R. Martin, Minister.

--- - 1786   Huff, James, and Biddy Woodey. William Lovell, Minister.

Nov. 17, 1783   Huff, Joseph, and Sarah Richmond. John Newman, Minister.

Oct. 26, 1828   Hughes, Madison R., and Sarah S. Dillard. Maning Hill, Minister.

Return for 1790 & 1791   Hughs, Robt., and Mary Lacky. Robert Jones, Minister.

July 18, 1805   Humphry, Morriss, and Disey Long. Maning Hill, Minister.

Jan. 2, 1824   Hundley, George, and Emblam M. Lovell. Othniel Minter, Minister.

Jan. 3, 1844   Hundley, Granville, and Louisa Odle. Othneil Minter, Minister.

Dec. 16, 1841   Hundley, Josiah, and Emily Lysle.

Dec. 24, 1838   Hundley, William, and Nancy Lyle. John D. Hankins, Minister.

Return for 1790 & 1791   Hunt, Moses, and Mary Brannam. Robert Jones, Minister.

Return dated 1833   Jackson, James, and Julia Craig. Silas Minter, Minister.

Apr. 19, 1846   Jackson, James, and Laura Eckhols. John Rich, Minister.

Mar. 5, 1782   Jameson, Joseph, and Sally Hubbard. Peter Smith, Minister.

Returns show   Jameson, Wm., and Elizabeth McWilliams. Michael
Oct. 1, 1781,   Dillingham, Minister.
to Mar. 20, 1782

Feb. 29, 1844   Jarrett, Robert, and Teresee Teel. William Schoolfield, Minister.

Nov. 16, 1837   Jennings, Swafford W., and Betsy G. Farris. Othniel Minter, Minister.

Feb. - 1833   Jimmerson, John H., and Jane Spencer. Silas Minter, Minister.

Return dated   Jinkings, Joseph, and Patsy Griffin. Maning Hill,
Oct. 29, 1819   Minister.

June 24, 1792   Joice, (Andrew), and Elizabeth King. Joseph Anthony, Minister.

Dec. 29, 1829   Johns, Anthony B., and Eliza M. Rieves. Nathan Anderson, Minister.

Dec. 22, 1825   Jones, Armistead, and Cassandra Barrow. Arnold Walker, Minister.

Feb. 10, 1817   Jones, Austin, and Ruth Shelton. John C. Taylor, Minister.

July - 1831   Jones, Bird, and Mary Roach. Arnold Walker, Minister.

Mar. 24, 1818   Jones, Buckner, and Hannah Martin. Maning Hill, Minister.

Dec. 17, 1835   Jones, Daniel, and Scinthy Harris. William Davis, Minister.

Dec. 13, 1828   Jones, George, and Ann King. Edwin G. Cabaniss, Minister.

Dec. 23, 1830   Jones, Greenwood, and Rachel Dyer. Richard Beck, Minister.

May 1, 1839   Jones, John A., and Susan Agee. Othniel Minter, Minister.

May - 1839   Jones, John A., and Susan Age.

Nov. 4, 1789   Jones, John, and Cealey Cesterson. Joseph Anthony, Minister.

Mar. - 1838   Jones, Joseph M., and Margaret C. Davis. Arnold Walker, Minister.

Dec. 21, 1823   Jones, Willis, and Mary George. Maning Hill, Minister.

Jan. 3, 1833	Jones, Wm., and Elizabeth Hardy. Othniel Minter, Minister.
Returns dated Aug. 24, 1790	Jonston, James, and Joice Wells. Carter Tarrant, Minister.
Apr. 1, 1830	Kallum, Horatio, and Abegail Burrus. Maning, Hill, Minister.
Dec. 24, 1829	Kallum, John, and Nancy Burrus. Maning Hill, Minister.
Jan. 1, 1784	Keaton, Zachariah, and Elizabeth Adams. John Newman, Minister.
Dec. 25, 1806	Kelly, Mason, and Sarah Chowning. James Patterson, Minister.
Return dated 1835	Kennerly, John, and E. Cheatham. John C. Traylor, Minister.
Dec. 28, 1809	Kilso, James, and Karon Kea. James Patterson, Minister.
Feb. 10, 1848	Kindrick, John, and Mary Agee. Daniel G. Taylor, Minister.
Dec. 12, 1829	King, Columbus, and Maria Cahill. Edwin G. Cabaniss, Minister.
Oct. 14, 1829	King, George, and Mary Cahill. Oth. Minter, Minister.
Apr. 7, 1822	King, John, and Elizabeth Waller. John C. Taylor, Minister.
Dec. 19, 1811	King, Joseph, and Dolly Clanton. William Davis, Minister.
Dec. 16, 1785	King, Stephen, and Lewany Maupine. Joseph Anthony, Minister.
May 17, 1787	King, Thomas, and Nancy Waller. Joseph Anthony, Minister.
July 24, 1794	King, William, and Nancy Mitchell. Clement Nance, Minister.
Feb. 10, 1817	Kington, Joseph, and Ailse Suttonfield. John C. Taylor, Minister.
July 26, 1826	Kington, Reuben, and Sarah Burchet. Othniel Minter, Minister.
Dec. 15, 1792	Kirkman, Wm., and Elizabeth Blize. Joseph Anthony, Minister.
Apr. 7, 1822	Kyle, James, and Elizabeth Jones. John C. Taylor, Minister.

Jan. 14, 1847   Lamkin, James, and Louisa Norman. Arthur W. Eanes, Minister.

July 4, 1833   Lamkin, Richard G., and Ann P. Bouldin. A. Walker, Minister.

Aug. 1, 1826   Land, Samuel, and Elizabeth Gilley. William Davis, Minister.

Oct. 12, 1825   Land, William, and Lydia Wilson. Arnold Walker, Minister.

Mar. 5, 1807   Larison, James, and Nancy Norman. James Patterson, Minister.

Sept. 20, 1821   Larison, Peter, and Janet Cox. William Davis, Minister.

Dec. 27, 1833   Lavender, Jesse, and Jane Davis. Othniel Minter, Minister.

Nov. 6, 1845   Law, David F., and Averilla Law. John R. Martin, Minister.

Mar. 4, 1792   Lawless, Jesse, and Agniss Dillian. Joseph Anthony, Minister.

Dec. 30, 1830   Lawrence, Arthur F., and Polly Pearson. Richard Beck, Minister.

Nov. 12, 1846   Lawrence, James H., and Ann Smith.

Jan. 12, 1832   Lawrence, James H., and Elizabeth Pearson. Richard B. Beck, Minister.

Oct. 14, 1817   Leak, Garland, and Mary Rea. Maning Hill, Minister.

Feb. 20, 1826   Leak, Garland, and Harriet Doyel. Othniel Minter, Minister.

Oct. 26, 1792   Leathworth, Benjamin, and Ellenor Addams. Joseph Anthony, Minister.

May 27, 1821   Leffel, Thos., and Sedney Burchett. Othneil Minter, Minister.

Oct. 19, 1839   Lester, Jesse, and America Trent. Othniel Minter, Minister.

Feb. - 1839   Lester, Daniel, and Nancy Hicks. Arnold Walker, Minister.

Nov. 12, 1840   Lewis, Demarquis, and Arrenia Clifton. Arthur W. Eanes, Minister.

Dec. 25, 1791   Lindsey, Henry, and Elizabeth Smith. Joseph Anthony, Minister.

Mar. 5, 1829	Lindsey, James, and Nancy Smith. Arnold Walker, Minister.
Aug. 7, 1821	Linsey, John, and Polly Ray. William Davis, Minister.
Jan. 16, 1783	Little, George, and Mary Cooper. Nathan Hall, Minister.
June 5, 1782	Lockhart, Thos., and Polley Taylor. Nathan Hall, Minister.
Feb. 17, 1807	Long, Gabriel, and Salley Humphreys. Maning Hill, Minister.
--- 20, 1783	Long, Thomas, and ----- -----. Peter Smith, Minister.
May 1, 1783	Lovell, John, and Mary Harbour. By Publication. John Newman, Minister.
May - 1847	Lovell, John J., and Rhoda Heard. John R. Martin, Minister.
Return dated Nov. 20, 178-?	Low, Stephen, and Ruth Kearby. Michael Dillingham, Minister.
Apr. 16, 1783	Loyd, John, and Sarah Smith. Nathan Hall, Minister.
Return dated 1830	Loyd, Thomas, and Nancy Higgs. John C. Traylor, Minister.
July 17, 1834	Mackdanneal, Stephen, and Fanny Wilson.
Mar. 20, 1783	Makenney, Elexander, and Mary Polsten. Nathan Hall, Minister.
Feb. 16, 1809	Mayho, John, and Judith Corn. Mannin Hill, Minister.
Jan. 13, 1831	Maynor, John, and Martha McBride. John Turner, Minister.
Undated	Mayo, Thomas, and Mary Blair. William Lovell, Minister.
Return for 1790 & 1791	Mayo, Volentine, and Martha Hughs. Robert Jones, Minister.
Return for 1790 & 1791	Mayo, William James, and Elizabeth Hancock. Robert Jones, Minister.
Nov. 7, 1783	Mays, Henry, and Rachel Bridges. John Newman, Minister.
Return dated Nov. 9, 1847	Mahon, Reuben, and Virginia Harris. Joseph H. Eanes, Minister.

Nov. 6, 1828   Mahon, William, and Sarah Briant. William Davis, Minister.

--- - 1786   Mainyar, John, and Elizabeth Burnet. William Lovell, Minister.

Return dated   Major, James, and Nancy Abington. John C. Traylor, Jan. 23, 1818   Minister.

Dec. - 1832   Majors, Roland, and Martha Willson. Silas Minter, Minister.

Oct. 18, 1828   Mann, William, and Betsey Stewart. Othniel Minter, Minister.

Feb. 24, 1831   Manning, Joshua, and Martha Frazier. John Turner, Minister.

Oct. 22, 1799   Manor, Jeremiah, and Nancy Miller. Saml. King, Minister.

Dec. 3, 1799   Manor, Stephen, and Polly Cradick. Saml. King, Minister.

Jan. 12, 1821   Marrick, Edward, and Martha Smith. John C. Traylor, Minister.

Dec. 29, 1840   Marshal, Whittington, and Catherine McDaniel. Arthur W. Eanes, Minister.

Return dated   Marshall, Elias, and Frances West. Maning Hill, May 8, 1819   Minister.

May 24, 1820   Marshall, James, and Susanah Weaver. Maning Hill, Minister.

July 3, 1849   Marshall, John W., and Eliza Ann Dunavant. George W. McNeely, Minister.

Mar. 27, 1828   Marshall, James, and Jane S. Doyle. Othneil Minter, Minister.

(Mar. 27, 1828) Marshall, James, and (Jane T. Doyle).

June 25, 1835   Marshall, Madison, and Virginia Lane. William Davis, Minister.

May 7, 1838   Martain, Jesse, and Matilda Bryan. Othniel Minter, Minister.

--- - 1783   Martain, William, and Magdelin Davy (?). Wm. Lovell, Minister.

Nov. 24, 1824   (Martin), Abner, and Jane Jones. Orson Martin, Minister.

Feb. 6, 1827   Martin, Constant, and Judith Turner. John Turner, Minister.

Return dated 1830	Martin, George W., and Elizabeth Starling. John C. Traylor, Minister.
June 12, 1827	Martin, Isaac, and Elizabeth Smith. Joshua Adams, Minister.
Undated	Martin, Joseph, and ----- -----. (Bond mutilated)
Oct. 24, 1826	Martin, Orson, and Mary Jones. Orson Martin, Minister.
Return dated 1837	Martin, Richard, and Lucy Taylor. John C. Traylor, Minister.
Apr. 13, 1819	Mason, Carter, and Elizabeth Moore. Othniel Minter, Minister.
Aug. 2, 1792	Mastin, Jacob, and Luise Melvin. Joseph Anthony, Minister.
Nov. - 1841	Mathews, Coleman, and Mildred Egleton. A. Walker, Minister.
Return dated 1835	Matthews, Dabney W., and Lucy Matthews. Silas Minter, Minister.
Jan. 1, 1824	Mathews, James, and Eliza Allen. John C. Traylor, Minister.
Aug. 28, 1827	Mathews, William, and Mary S. Staples. Bird Lowe, Minister.
Return dated 1837	Matthews, -----, and Lucy Mullins. John C. Traylor, Minister.
Return dated June 25, 1844	Mathis, Claiborne, and Jane Egleton. Joseph H. Eanes, Minister.
Feb. 13, 1817	Mattock, William, and Ruth Atkerson. Maning Hill, Minister.
Nov. 16, 1847	Maxey, Levi, and Martha Ann Good. David Good, father. Wm. Schoolfield, Minister.
Jan. 6, 1829	McBride, Jacob, and Dessa Wills. Othneil Minter, Minister.
Oct. 13, 1790	McBride, John, and Nancy Brammer. Randolph Hall, Minister.
Return for 1797	McCullar, Ellexander, and Susanner Nance. John King, Minister.
Jan. 29, 1832	McDaniel, James, and Elizabeth Goodman. Richard B. Beck, Minister.
Apr. 4, 1836	McDaniel, John, and Pheba Sampson. Othniel Minter, Minister.

Nov. 27, 1842   McDonald, Beckworth, and Jenetta Wilson.
                 Arthur W. Eanes, Minister.

Apr. 14, 1847   McDonald, Robert, and Mary Cahall. Arthur W. Eanes,
                 Minister.

Aug. 1, 1787   McKinney, John, and Delilah Winney. Joseph Anthony,
                 Minister.

Feb. 10, 1817   McLean, William, and Caroline House. John C. Taylor,
                 Minister.

Oct. 14, 1833   McMillen, Joseph, and Elizabeth Shoemate. Othniel Minter,
                 Minister.

Dec. 13, 1829   McMillion, William, and Ann Watkins. Maning Hill,
                 Minister.

Aug. 11, 1831   Means, Thomas P., and Dicey Fee. Maning Hill,
                 Minister.

--- - 1783   MecKinsey, John, and Isbel Hix. Wm. Lovell, Minister.

Jan. 12, 1826   Meeks, Coleman, and Susannah Jones. William Davis,
                 Minister.

Dec. 5, 1822   Menzoes, John C., and Pamelia Jones. William Davis,
                 Minister.

Jan. 6, 1786   Meshew, Jacob, and Mary Lindsay. Joseph Anthony.

Oct. 6, 1842   Millner, Marquiss D. L., and Sarah Ann Tinsley.
                 Arthur W. Eanes, Minister.

July 29, 1845   Millner, Thomas F., and Mary Ann Tinsley.
                 W. N. Mebane, Minister.

Oct. 31, 1848   Mills, Aaron, and Mary Young. Wm. M. Schoolfield,
                 Minister.

Dec. 19, 1844   Mills, Richard, and Judith Poindexter.

Nov. - 1832   Mills, Robert, and Catharine Floyd. Silas Minter, Minister.

Dec. 7, 1845   Mills, William, and Martha Mills.

Return dated   Mils, James, and Elizabeth Oakley. Silas Minter,
1833   Minister.

Return dated   Minter, Johnson, and Susan Clark. Silas Minter, Minister.
1835

Jan. 13, 1842   Minter, Joseph, and Nancy Norman. Arthur W. Eanes,
                 Minister.

Nov. 19, 1846   Minter, Joseph, and Margaret Davis. Jeremiah Bonnett,
                 Minister.

June - 1837	Minter, Othniel, and Mary Burgess. Arnold Walker, Minister.
Nov. 26, 1840	Minter, Richard W., and Mary Ann Doyle.
Apr. - 1845	Minter, Silas, and Betsey Philpott. A. Walker, Minister.
Oct. - 1846	Minter, Silas, and Jane A. Eggleton. A. Walker, Minister.
Dec. - 1842	Mitchel, John C., and Elizabeth Napier. A. Walker, Minister.
Return dated June 25, 1844	Mitchell, Archibald W., and Sarah O. Norman. Joseph H. Evans, Minister.
Nov. 14, 1844	Mitchell, Ignatius F., and Lucy Jane Holt.
Sept. 26, 1845	Mitchell, Joel S., and Balzora Bouldin. Othniel Minter, Minister.
Return dated Mar. 18, 1815	Montgomery, John, and Elizabeth Jones. William Davis, Minister.
--- - 1838	Mooman, Edward, and Sally Bird. John C. Traylor, Minister.
Aug. 27, 1828	Moore, Thomas, and Frances Rea. Maning Hill, Minister.
Sept. 22, 1837	Moore, William B., and Nancy Mays. Othniel Minter, Minister.
Oct. 18, 1848	Morris, John W., and Elizabeth Mitchell. Wm. M. Schoolfield, Minister.
Return dated 1835	Morris, Joseph A., and Narcissa B. Aistrop. Silas Minter, Minister.
Nov. 20, 1823	Morris, Samuel, and Lucy Adams. Richard B. Beck, Minister.
Nov. 15, 1806	Morriss, William, and Tabitha Cheatham. Maning Hill, Minister.
Return for 1790 & 1791	Morrow, Matthew, and Fanny Burnett. Robert Jones, Minister.
Dec. 15, 1842	Mullen, James, and Martha Ann Wells. Wm. M. Schoolfield, Minister.
Mar. 22, 1788	Murphy, Clement, and Mary Jones. Joseph Anthony, Minister.
Feb. 4, 1783	Murphy, Joseph, and Susanah Morris. Nathan Hall, Minister.
--- - 1786	Murrow, David, and Elizabeth Murrow. William Lovell, Minister.

Aug. 30, 1846	Nance, Fontaine, and Jemima Grant. Geo. W. McNeely, Minister.
May 13, 1847	Nance, Henry, and Mary Ann Land. Arthur W. Eanes, Minister.
Undated	Nance, John, and Betty Ryan. Philip Ryan, father.
--- - 1786	Nevell, John, and Rachel Martin. William Lovell, Minister.
Mar. - 1832	Nichols. Greenbury, and America Spencer. Silas Minter, Minister.
Mar. 2, 1843	Norman, Courtney W., and Elizabeth J. Mitchell. Arthur W. Eanes, Minister.
Nov. 14, 1842	Norman, J. B., and Lucy W. Price. Othniel Minter, Minister.
Return dated Aug. 30, 1795	Northcut, Francis, and Lucy Hailey. John King, Minister.
May 25, 1835	Nunly, Thomas, and Eliza Wilson. William Davis, Minister.
Jan. 1, 1824	Nunn, Joel, and Sally Clark. John C. Traylor, Minister.
Feb. 14, 1831	Nunn, John, and Jane Davis. John Turner, Minister.
Oct. - 1845	Nunn, Riley, and Jane Thomasson. A. Walker, Minister.
Oct. - 1838	Nunn, Stephen, and Louisa Edwards. Arnold Walker, Minister.
Nov. 7, 1848	Oakley, Thomas, and Sarah Wells. Wm. M. Schoolfield, Minister.
June 7, 1832	Oakley, Washington, and Polley Evans. Manning Hill, Minister.
Sept. 1, 1836	Oakley, William M., and Iezpeand Mills. Othniel Minter, Minister.
Return dated July 12, 1842	Odell, Joseph, and Elizabeth Anderson. George W. -----, Minister.
Jan. 6, 1842	Odle, James, and Serena Gilley.
Jan. 13, 1845	Odle, William W., and Caroline M. Gilley. Othniel Minter, Minister.
--- - 1783	Okley, James, and Janet MacKiney. Wm. Lovell, Minister.

Return dated Mar. 18, 1815	Oldham, William, and Peggy Clarke. William Davis, Minister.
--- - 1783	O'Neal, Basil, and Ellener Briscoe. Wm. Lovell, Minister.
Jan. - 1846	Oxley, Alfred, and Sally Good. A. Walker, Minister.
Mar. 3, 1825	Pace, Daniel, and Jane King. Arnold Walker, Minister.
Undated	Pace, Francis, and Mariah Griggs.
Mar. 14, 1828	Pace, Francis, and Sarah Deshazo. Othniel Minter, Minister.
Aug. 2, 1847	Pace, Greenville T., and Lucy C. Trotter. John Rich, Minister.
Dec. 17, 1829	Pace, Heartwell, and Nancy Alland. Richard B. Beck, Minister.
Sept. 11, 1828	Pace, James B., and Caroline Hunter. Arnold Walker, Minister.
Jan. 26, 1847	Pace, James B., and Lucy E. Taylor. Wm. M. Schoolfield, Minister.
Return dated Nov. 20, 178-?	Pace, Joel, and Mary East. Michael Dillingham, Minister.
Sept. 3, 1832	Pace, Newson, Jr., and Parthena Maupin. Othniel Minter, Minister.
--- - 180-?	Pace, Thomas, and Nancy Webb.
Feb. 22, 1820	Palmer, Elijah, of Halifax County, and Coatney Casada. Richard B. Beck, Minister.
Jan. 20, 1814	Parish, Allen, and Frances Hunt. William Blair, Minister.
Nov. 6, 1786	Parting, James, and Frances Cornwell. Joseph Anthony, Minister.
Oct. 19, 1791	Patrick, James, and Sarah Dunlap. Andrew Hunter, Minister.
Undated	Patterson, Jarrott, and Lucy Payne. Silas Minter, Minister.
July 26, 1826	Payne, John, and Fanny Thomasson. Othniel Minter, Minister.
Dec. 23, 1844	Payne, Reyland, and Margaret E. Cox. Othniel Minter, Minister.
Returns show Oct. 1, 1781, to Mar. 20, 1782.	Payne, Rubin, and Ann Ray. Michael Dillingham, Minister.

Feb. 25, 1830	Payne, William, and Letty Ann Bouldin. Maning Hill, Minister.
Oct. 20, 1785	Peak, George, and Dinah Luttrell. Robert Jones, Minister.
Oct. 15, 1835	Pearson, James, and Rebecca Mathews. Orson Martin, Minister.
Return dated Aug. 30, 1795	Pearson, Meredith, and Roady DeLozar. John King, Minister.
Return dated 1830	Pearson, Peyton, and Polly Smith. John C. Traylor, Minister.
Jan. 6, 1814	Phifer, Forrest, and Susanna Philpott. Lewis Foster, Minister.
Oct. - 1839	Philips, William, and Martha M. Smith. Arnold Walker, Minister.
Jan. 1, 1824	Phillips, Alexander, and Sally Dillen. John C. Traylor, Minister.
Undated	Phillips, Gabriel, and Milley Reil. Wm. Lovell, Minister.
--- - 1783	Philpot, John, and Nancey Posey. Wm. Lovell, Minister.
Return dated July 27, 1806	Philpott, Allen, and Mary Ann Philpott. John King, Minister.
Jan. 1, 1824	Philpott, Charles, and Polly Bassett. John C. Traylor, Minister.
Return dated Nov. 11, 1811	Philpott, David, and Sarah Nance. James Patterson, Minister.
Sept. 12, 1826	Philpott, David, and Diannah Cahill. Othniel Minter, Minister.
Jan. 29, 1811	Philpott, John W., and Elizabeth Dillion. Lewis Foster, Minister.
Return dated 1835	Philpott, John J., and Elizabeth R. Walker. Silas Minter, Minister.
Aug. - 1847	Philpott, John T., and Mary E., -----. A. Walker, Minister.
Oct. - 1836	Philpott, Samuel, and Margaret Pyrtle. Arnold Walker, Minister.
June 20, 1782	Piatt, Ebenezer, and Rebecca Vincent (?). Nathan Hall, Minister.
July 23, 1828	Pierce, Harrison, and Nancy Clinkscales. Maning Hill, Minister.

Return dated 1836	Poindexter, John, and Louisa Mills. John C. Traylor, Minister.
Mar. 23, 1824	Porter, Bonepart, and Caty Oaks. William Davis, Minister.
Sept. 4, 1825	Porter. Gideon, and Jemima Rea. John C. Traylor, Minister.
Jan. 17,1789	Posey, Thomas, and Sarah Hubert. Joseph Anthony, Minister.
Dec. 13, 1830	Potter, William, and ----- Dillard. Consent only. "General John Dillard has no objection."
Nov. 16, 1825	Prat, John, and Trifina Stratton. Arnold Walker, Minister.
Sept. 8, 1783	Prater, Isaac, and Deborah Samples. John Newman, Minister.
Undated	Pratt, Felix, and Patience Wells. Silas Minter, Minister.
Sept. 20, 1831	Pratt, Felix, and Mary Roberson. Silas Minter, Minister.
Jan. 9, 1840	Prewit, Elijah, and An Clanton. John D. Hankins, Minister.
Return dated 1836	Price, -----, and -----Lanier. John C. Traylor, Minister.
Dec. 21, 1826	Price, Duke, and Rachel Trent. William Davis, Minister.
Return dated Feb. 11, 1839	Price, Duke, and Harriet M. Shackleford. Silas Minter, Minister.
Dec. - 1844	Price, James, and Mary E. Cahill. A. Walker, Minister.
May 12, 1825	Price, John, and Lucy Pratt. Arnold Walker, Minister.
July 14, 1842	Price, John, and Lucy W. Harris. Othniel Minter, Minister.
Jan. 5, 1846	Price, Rice, and Lusinda Moore. Geo W. McNeely, Minister.
Return dated 1835	Price, Williamson, and Frances Baker. John C. Traylor, Minister.
Return dated Nov. 9, 1847	Price, Zeed, and Eliza Lemon. Joseph H. Eanes, Minister.
Feb. 25, 1807	Proctor, Lewis, and Joyce Haley. James Patterson, Minister.

May 28, 1844	Pulliam, Drury, and Parthena Clanton. Arthur W. Eanes, Minister.
Return dated 1830	Purdy, Anderson, and Lucy Maupin. John C. Traylor, Minister.
July - 1832	Purdy, Anderson, and Cynthia Stults. Silas Minter, Minister.
Mar. 25, 1825	Purkins, William, and Martha Redd. John C. Taylor, Minister.
Return dated 1830	Purkins, Wm., and Martha Fontaine. John C. Traylor, Minister.
Apr. 19, 1835	Pulliam, William, and Sarah Goodman. Othniel Minter, Minister.
Apr. 9, 1835	Pyrtle, John D., and Elizabeth Lawrence. Othniel Minter, Minister.
Feb. 21, 1821	Peddigo, Henry, and Vilinda Poston. Othneil Minter, Minister.
Sept. 9, 1824	Peddigo, John, and Charity Poston. Othneil Minter, Minister.
Feb. - 1845	Peddigo, Henry S., and Mary Ann Smith. A. Walker, Minister.
Mar. 17, 1836	Pedigo, Henry M., and Mary A. Wells. Othniel Minter, Minister.
Oct. - 1845	Pedigo, John S., and Elizabeth Shumate. A. Walker, Minister.
Jan. 5, 1792	Pedigo, Robert, and Polly Parsley. Joseph Anthony, Minister.
Jan. 1, 1788	Pelphrey, Joseph, and Elizabeth Qualls. Joseph Anthony, Minister.
Return dated Nov. 15, ----	Penn, James, and Mary Shelton. Maning Hill, Minister.
Sept. 1, 1829	Perkins, Jessee, and Mary Fontaine. Nathan Anderson, Minister.
Oct. 13, 1825	Perkinson, Hesekiah, and Susannah Philpott. Arnold Walker, Minister.
Jan. 25, 1825	Perkinson, William, and ---ba Lawrence. Orson Martin, Minister.
Undated	Perry, Thomas, and Agnes Crowley. William Lovell, Minister.
Nov. 5, 1849	Peters, Henry D., and Mary F. Gravley. R. P. Bibb, Minister.

Feb. 25, 1836	Petty, Davis, and Sary Childers. William Davis, Minister.
July 25, 1849	Petty, Isham M., and Mary Evins. Balaam Warren, Minister.
Apr. 24, 1792	Qualls, John, and Jerisha Ferriss. Joseph Anthony, Minister.
Nov. 23, 1791	Quarles, James, and Elizabeth Pelphry. Joseph Anthony, Minister.
Aug. 11, 1825	Rainey, Daniel, and Susan Starling. John C. Traylor, Minister.
Nov. 12, 1832	Ramey, James, and Elizabeth Davis. Othniel Minter, Minister.
Jan. 13, 1833	Ramsey, Thos., and Winefred Davis. Othniel Minter, Minister.
Oct. - 1838	Ramsey, Woodson, and Mary C. Davis. Arnold Walker, Minister.
Oct. 25, 1790	Ratliff, Silar, and Fanny Hancock. Randolph Hall, Minister.
Dec. - 1824	Ray, Brice W., and Nancy S. Ramy. Arnold Walker, Minister.
Return dated Mar. 18, 1815	Ray, James, and Judith Francis. William Davis, Minister.
Mar. 7, 1826	Rea, Bruce, and Polly Cox. Arnold Walker, Minister.
Jan. 28, 1830	Rea, Edmund J., and Pamelia J. Clinkscales. Maning Hill, Minister.
Sept. 14, 1841	Rea, Iredell J., and Virginia Salman. Wm. H. Schoolfield, Minister.
Jan. - 1827	Rea, James, and Elizabeth Hewlett. Arnold Walker, Minister.
Nov. 12, 1816	Rea, Joseph, and Mary West. Maning Hill, Minister.
Dec. 23, 1831	Rea, John B., and Biddy Moore, Silas Minter, Minister.
July 31, 1849	Reamy, Peter R., and Sarah J. Waller. Wm. M. Schoolfield, Minister.
Nov. 27, 1785	Reaves, Burwell, and Mary Gillam. Robert Jones, Minister.
Nov. 21, 1825	Reay, Brice, and Nancy S. Ramy. Consent only. Lowes Ramy, mother.

Undated   Reel, George, and Nancy Ross. By Publication.
               Wm. Lovell, Minister.

Apr. 14, 1831 Rely, Daniel, and Lucinda Rea. Maning Hill, Minister.

--- - 1786   Rentfro, Joshua, and Jennet Hairstone. William Lovell,
               Minister.

Apr. 17, 1821 Reynolds, William, and Lucy Burchett. Othneil Minter,
               Minister.

Jan. 16, 1847 Reynolds, William N., and A---- Mills. Geo. W.
               McNeely, Minister.

Nov. 20, 1844 Rice, John D., and Eliza A. Gravely. Nathan Anderson,
               Minister.

July 6, 1790   Rice, Joseph, and Mary Prince Payne. Clement Nance,
               Minister.

Dec. 21, 1847 Rice, William R., and Sarah B. Nowlin, dau. of
               B. W. Nowlin. Samul Davis Rice, Minister.

Dec. 20, 1838 Richardson, Abner, and Nancy Minter. Othniel Minter,
               Minister.

Aug. 8, 1839   Richardson, Arthur, and Mary J. Fleeman. Nathan
               Anderson, Minister.

Nov. 20, 1834 Richardson, George, and Clarissa Martin. Othniel
               Martin, Minister.

Dec. - 1839   Richardson, John, and Susan Lester. Arnold Walker,
               Minister.

Returns dated Richerson, Edward, and Sarah Thomason. Carter
Aug. 24, 1790 Tarrant, Minister.

Oct. 28, 1786 Richerson, Thos., and Clery Dun. Joseph Anthony,
               Minister.

June 6, 1833   Rickman, Nicolas, and Ruth Harris. Othniel Minter,
               Minister.

May - 1832   Riley, Daniel, and Nancy Franklin. Silas Minter, Minister.

Feb. 2, 1840   Roach, James, and Metilda Cayton.

Dec. 25, 1825 Roberts, James, and Ann Meredith. Othniel Minter,
               Minister.

Dec. 22, 1825 Roberts, James, and Ann Meredith. Othniel Minter,
               Minister.

Apr. 25, 1791 Roberts, Samuel, and Patience Worhell (?). Andrew
               Hunter, Minister.

Oct. 27, 1839	Robertson, James C., and Mary Lewis. Othniel Minter, Minister.
Apr. 11, 1786	Rogers, William, and Roesey Heard. Joseph Anthony, Minister.
June - 1824	Rogers, William and Susannah Perdie. Arnold Walker, Minister.
Jan. 12, 1821	Rowland, Creed, and Matilda Brewer. John C. Traylor, Minister.
Nov. 6, 1788	Rowland, Baldy, and Elizabeth Carpenter. Joseph Anthony, Minister.
Dec. 16, 1838	Royster, Banister, and Martha Terrell. Othniel Minter, Minister.
Return dated July 27, 1806	Runnolds, John, and Sarah Philpott. John King, Minister.
Dec. 20, 1825	Salmon, James D., and Elizabeth Maupin. Othniel Minter, Minister.
Aug. 18, 1833	Salmon, John, and Eliza Clanton. A. Walker, Minister.
Feb. 23, 1832	Salmon, Thaddius, and America Pyrtle. Othniel Minter, Minister.
Jan. 18, 1792	Salmons, Hezekiah, and Mary Fortune. Joseph Anthony, Minister.
Jan. 13, 1842	Samms, Elijah, and Caroline Watkins.
July 20, 1834	Sams, Jeams, and Amelia Clavil.
Jan. 1, 1824	Saunders, -----, and Nancy Staples. John C. Traylor, Minister.
June 1, 1828	Scales, John P., and Judith Shelton. Maning Hill, Minister.
Sept. 21, 1834	Scales, Peter, and Lucinda Leek. John Washburn, Minister.
Oct. 30, 1783	Scurlock, James, and Lidy Poore. John Newman, Minister.
Dec. 31, 1833	Shackelford, Wm., and Abigail Taylor. Othniel Minter, Minister.
Mar. 14, 1809	Shackleford, Henry, and Barshaba Agee. James Patterson, Minister.
Nov. 28, 1848	Sheffield, William A., and Catharine M. Hill. Wm. M. Schoolfield, Minister.

Return dated July 27, 1806	Shelton, James, and Fanney Allen. John King, Minister.
Mar. - 1832	Shelton, Peter, and Magdelene Watkins. Silas Minter, Minister.
Oct. - 1836	Shoemake, Westly, and Josephine Pyrtle. Arnold Walker, Minister.
Dec. - 1841	Shumate, Daniel, and Elizabeth Pace. A. Walker, Minister.
Feb. - 1846	Shumate, Samuel, and Nancy Pace. A. Walker, Minister.
Aug. 14, 1820	Silliman, John, and ----- -----. (Presbyterian)
Returns dated Aug. 24, 1790	Sims, Ignatious, and Jane Nance. Carter Tarrant, Minister.
Feb. 15, 1783	Sims, James, and Elizabeth Sims. Nathan Hall, Minister.
Jan. 11, 1827	Sims, John D., and Lucy Baker. Othniel Minter, Minister.
June 15, 1782	Sims, Matthew, and Jane Moore. Nathan Hall, Minister.
Nov. 24, 1845	Singleton, William, and America Anne Meade. Wellington E. Webb, Minister.
Return for 1790 & 1791	Small, Thomas, and Elizabeth Burnett. Robert Jones, Minister.
Sept. 25, 1831	Smith, Abner, and Elizabeth Hill. Maning Hill, Minister.
Nov. 26, 1836	Smith, Brice, and Jane Thomasson. Othniel Minter, Minister.
May 8, 1783	Smith, Caleb, and Keziah Holt. By Publication. John Newman, Minister.
Oct. 20, 1786	Smith, Caleb, and Sarah Holmns. Joseph Anthony, Minister.
Apr. 7, 1822	Smith, Dabney, and Mary Melvin (?). John C. Taylor, Minister.
Return dated Feb. 11, 1839	Smith, Daniel D., and Lucy B. Minter. Silas Minter, Minister.
Mar. 26, 1845	Smith, David, and Sarah Dunavant. Othniel Minter, Minister.
Mar. 26, 1845	Smith, David, and Sarah Dunnavant.
Aug. 8, 1783	Smith, Elijah, and Margaret Preston. By Publication. John Newman, Minister.

Return dated May 27, 1784	Smith, Gideon, and Mary -----. William Lovell, Minister.
Dec. 24, 1847	Smith, Hiram, and Nancy J. Clemmons. Daniel G. Taylor, Minister.
Mar. 9, 1788	Smith, John, and Salthiel Spencer. Joseph Anthony, Minister.
Mar. 25, 1825	Smith, John, and Betsy Jimmerson (?). John C. Taylor, Minister.
Jan. 1, 1824	Smith, Joseph, and Nancy Dillen. John C. Traylor, Minister.
Apr. 5, 1832	Smith, William, and America Briant. William Davis, Minister.
Dec. 24, 1833	Smith, William, and Elizabeth McMillen. Othniel Minter, Minister.
Undated	Snell, James F., and Polly Turner. License dated Apr. 30, 1839.
May 1, 1839	Snell, James F., and Polley Turner. Othniel Minter, Minister.
Return dated July - 1809	Snider, Christian, and Sally Turner. Lewis Foster, Minister.
Return dated 1836	Southall, William, and E. Watkins. John C. Traylor, Minister.
June 4, 1783	Spencer, John, and Sarah Lynch. By Publication. John Newman, Minister.
Mar. 22, 1835	Spencer, Nathaniel, and Martha Dyer. Arnold Walker, Minister.
Undated	Stamp, George, and Mary Haul. By Publication. Wm. Lovell, Minister.
July 2, 1802	Staples, George, and Caroline Stowball. Joseph Anthony, Minister.
Sept. 16, 1844	Staples, H. H., and Margaret Hereford. Consent only. John L. Hereford, parent.
Sept. 24, 1844	Staples, Harden H., and Margaret E. Hereford, John Rich, Minister.
June 21, 1826	Staples, John C., and Mary M. Martin. Arnold Walker, Minister.
May 22, 1803	Starling, Thomas, and Anny Redd. Joseph Anthony, Minister.
Jan. - 1839	Steagall, Alfred, and Ann King. Arnold Walker, Minister.

Feb. 6, 1832	Stephens, Coleman, and Jane Fee. John Washburn, Minister.
Return dated Jan. 23, 1818	Stewart, David, and Ann Hancock. John C. Taylor, Minister.
Dec. 22, 1829	Stewart, David, and Mariah Grinsted. John Washurn, Minister.
Nov. 13, 1834	Stockton, Charles W., and Mary H. Barrow. Arnold Walker, Minister.
Jan. 4, 1781	Stockton, Richard, and Betsy Copeland. By Publication in Chesterfield Co. Peter Smith, Minister.
Oct. 13, 1835	Stokes, Allen, and Louisa Jones. William Davis, Minister.
Dec. 5, 1837	Stokes, German, and Matilda Hunt. Arthur W. Eanes, Minister.
Jan. 12, 1821	Stone, Daniel, and Elizabeth Dillard. John C. Traylor, Minister.
Jan. 3, 1828	Stone, Eusibious, and Elizabeth Draper. Othniel Minter, Minister.
(Jan. 3, 1828)	Stone, Eusabius, and ----- -----.
Return dated Nov. 9, 1847	Stone, James, and Susan E. Martin (?). Joseph H. Eanes, Minister.
Mar. 9, 1788	Stone, John, and Elizabeth Spencer. Joseph Anthony, Minister.
Aug. 2, 1792	Stone, John, and Mary Philpott. Joseph Anthony, Minister.
Feb. 24, 1842	Stone, John P., and Lethia Mitchell. Arthur W. Eanes, Minister.
--- -- 1783	Stone, Micajer, and Martha Cesteson. Wm. Lovell, Minister.
Return dated 1790	Storms, Cornelis, and Nancy Burres. Jesse Rentfro, Minister.
Return dated 1837	Stovall, James K., and Louisinda Pace. John C. Traylor, Minister.
Returns show Oct. 1, 1781, to Mar. 20, 1782	Stovall, Thomas, and Elizabeth Cooper. Michael Dillingham, Minister.
Jan. 18, 1825	Stow, James, and Martha Nunn. John C. Traylor, Minister.
Mar. 11, 1845	Stratton, Joseph, and Elizabeth Stratton. Othniel Minter, Minister.

Apr. 1, 1846	Stratton, Joseph, and Elizabeth Stratton.
Aug. 24, 1837	Stratton, William J., and Arminda Mahon. Othniel Minter, Minister.
Dec. 15, 1783	Street, Wm., and Mary Stamps. John Newman, Minister.
June 22, 1792	Stuart, William, and Milly Estes. Joseph Anthony, Minister.
Return for 1797	Stulce, John, and Ann Melvin. John King, Minister.
Dec. 11, 1834	Stults, Anderson, and Polly Lester. Arnold Walker, Minister.
July - 1848	Stults, Benjamin E., and Sarah Jane Davis. A. Walker, Minister.
Dec. 19, 1850	Stults, Brice M., and Tamsy Ann Wells. Jno. R. Martin, Minister.
Jan. - 1824	Stults, Joseph, and Lucy Egelton. Arnold Walker, Minister.
Oct. 6, 1796	Sumpter, George, and Susanah Mayse. Wm. Heath, Minister.
Aug. 26, 1836	Sumpter, Geo., and Elizabeth Turner. Othniel Minter, Minister.
Mar. 10, 1792	Sumpter, William, and Pegnance Purtle. Joseph Anthony, Minister.
Return dated May 27, 1784	Sumter, John, and Elizabeth Chadwick. Publication. William Lovell, Minister.
Jan. 13, 1845	Suttenfield, James M., and Nancy G. Taylor. John Robertson, Minister.
Nov. - 1844	Stanley, Swinfield, and Lucinda Trent. A. Walker, Minister.
Dec. 10, 1782	Swinney, William, and Elizabeth How. Nathan Hall, Minister.
Mar. 1, 1836	Taylor, Geo. W., and Sarah H. Hailey. Othniel Minter, Minister.
Jan. 23, 1845	Taylor, George W., and Martha A. Shelton. John Robertson, Minister.
Return dated Feb. 11, 1839	Taylor, James M., and Martha Jane Stults. Silas Minter, Minister.
Return dated Feb. 11, 1839	Taylor, John, and Louisa M. Hankin. Silas Minter, Minister.

Oct. 13, 1842   Taylor, John P. H., and Ruth P. Baker,   John T. St. Clair, Minister.

Apr. 12, 1824   Taylor, Joseph, and Nancy Vawter. William Davis, Minister.

Dec. - 1837   Taylor, Robert, and Martha Minter. Arnold Walker, Minister.

Return dated   Taylor, Wm., and Catharine Hill. John C. Traylor, Jan. 23, 1818   Minister.

Nov. - 1838   Taylor, William D., and Julia Ann Lylle. Arnold Walker, Minister.

Dec. 11, 1828   Terry, Abner R., and Eleanor Dyer. Arnold Walker, Minister.

May 27, 1851   Terry, William P., and Mary E. King. W. N. Mebane, Minister.

Oct. 19, 1806   Thomason, Arnold, and Pheby Dyer. James Patterson, Minister.

Return dated   Thomason, Elias, and Elizabeth Barns. James Patterson, Nov. 11, 1811   Minister.

Returns dated   Thomason, Fleman, and ----- -----. Carter Tarrant, Aug. 24, 1790   Minister.

Oct. 18, 1830   Thomason, George, and Elizabeth Pace. Arnold Walker, Minister.

Dec. 7, 1827   Thomasson, Arnold, and Sarah Gothard. Orson Martin, Minister.

Dec. - 1846   Thomasson, George, and Julia Ann Coleman. A. Walker, Minister.

Nov. 9, 1826   Thomasson, John, and Lucy Thomasson. Othniel Minter, Minister.

Jan. - 1849   Thomerson, Presley, and Nancy Nunn. A. Walker, Minister.

Apr. 20, 1834   Thomerson, John, and Jane Robertson. A. Walker, Minister.

Nov. - 1838   Thomerson, William, and Nancy B. Turner. Arnold Walker, Minister.

Returns show   Thompson, Richard, and Charity Whitacer. Michael Oct. 1, 1781,   Dillingham, Minister. to Mar. 20, 1782

Mar. 25, 1825   Thompson, Waddy, and Mary Abington. John C. Taylor, Minister.

Aug. 31, 1826   Thornton, James, and Martha C. Royster. Arnold Walker, Minister.

--- - 1847	Thornton, Thomas J., and Adeline E. Thomas. A. Walker, Minister.
May 11, 1842	Tio, William, and Metilda E. Sumpter. Othniel Minter, Minister.
Sept. 30, 1844	Tolbert, Elisha, and Sarah Dyer. Arthur W. Eanes, Minister.
Mar. 12, 1844	Tolbert, John J., and Liza McDonald.
Return dated Mar. 30, 1820	Traviss, Abner, and Rachel B. Weaver. Maning Hill, Minister.
Jan. 31, 1832	Turner, Aron, and Texceney Bateman. Richard B. Beck, Minister.
Jan. 13, 1824	Turner, Constantine, and Elizabeth Pyrtle. Othniel Minter, Minister.
Sept. - 1838	Turner, James O., and Sarah Cahill. Arnold Walker, Minister.
Nov. 14, 1825	Turner, John. Ordination Bonds. Baptist.
July 1, 1830	Turner, Josiah, and Elizabeth Gilly. Richard B. Beck, Minister.
Jan. 16, 1789	Turner, Larkin, and Mary Hicks (?). Joseph Anthony, Minister.
Sept. 15, 1836	Turner, Marlin, and Salley Long. Othniel Minter, Minister.
Jan. 13, 1842	Turner, Meadows, and Eliza Jane Griffith. Arthur W. Eanes, Minister.
Sept. - 1842	Turner, Meshack, and Sarah Ann Deshazo. A. Walker, Minister.
June 25, 1834	Turner, Moses, and Marthy Rite. William Davis, Minister.
--- 18, 1806	Turner, Shours, and Addelpha Turner. Lewis Foster, Minister.
Dec. 4, 1828	Turner, Terry, and Nancy Gilly. William Davis, Minister.
Nov. - 1843	Turner, Whitfield, and Sarah Ann Martin. Arnold Walker, Minister.
Dec. 22, 1812	Turner, William, and Pheba Wilson. William Davis, Minister.
Dec. - 1837	Turner, William, and Martha Philpott. Arnold Walker, Minister.
June 8, 1846	Tush, Lewis G., and Matilda Moore. Geo. W. McNealy, Minister.
Sept. 13, 1838	Uhles, David, and Martha Prewit. John D. Hankins, Minister.

Jan. 12, 1831	Varnum, Ewell, and Weby Oakley. Silas Minter, Minister.
Nov. 5, 1810	Vaughan, Roberson, and Elizabeth Durham. Maning Hill, Minister.
June 18, 1782	Vaughn, Reubin, and Mary McKenny. By Publication. Peter Smith, Minister.
Dec. 30, 1810	Vauter, Bradford, and Patsey Taylor. Maning Hill, Minister.
Oct. 10, 1816	Vauter, Chadwell, and Susannah Taylor. Maning Hill, Minister.
Oct. 26, 1845	Vernon, James, and Sally Fisher.
Nov. 24, 1785	Vest, Peter, and Pugnance Vaughn. Joseph Anthony, Minister.
Nov. 17, 1846	Vier, James, of Patrick County, and Mary Baker. Joshua Adams, Minister.
Jan. 12, 1832	Wade, Joseph A., and Sarah S. Cheatham. Maning Hill, Minister.
Undated	Wade, Moses, and Faney Forgason. By License. Wm. Lovell, Minister.
Nov. - 1846	Wade, William, and Jane Bowles. A. Walker, Minister.
June - 1845	Waganer, Samuel H., and Elizabeth Hundley. A. Walker, Minister.
Dec. - 1842	Waggoner, John, and Ann Thomerson. A. Walker, Minister.
Aug. 10, 1782	Walden, William, and Catharine Foley. Nathan Hall, Minister.
Aug. 10, 1823	Walker, Arnold. Ordination Certificate. Presbyterian.
Nov. 21, 1786	Walker, Elijah, and Elizabeth Simmons. Joseph Anthony, Minister.
Dec. 24, 1845	Walker, Joseph L., and Lucy G. Hix. John R. Martin, Minister.
Dec. 21, 1809	Walker, William S., and Salley Norman. James Patterson, Minister.
Dec. 2, 1847	Wall, Claiborne D., and Elizabeth J. Smith. John R. Martin, Minister.
July 13, 1806	Waller, Carr, and Susanna Edwards. James Patterson, Minister.
Mar. - 1823	Waller, Edmond, and Ann King. John C. Traylor, Minister.

Return dated 1830	Waller, George, and Elizabeth Waller. John C. Traylor, Minister.
Oct. 26, 1841	Waller, James E., and Mary Fontaine. Wm. M. Schoolfield, Minister.
Sept. - 1841	Walton, Elisha, and Milly Stone. A. Walker, Minister.
July 10, 1849	Warren, Balaam, and Julia A. Barbour. ---- Austin, Minister.
--- - 1823	Warthen, Walter G., and Lucy A. Rea. Arnold Walker, Minister.
Mar. - 1836	Watkins, John D., and Jane A. G. Martin. Arnold Walker, Minister.
Sept. 17, 1844	Watkins, Peter W., and Louisa Hairston. Saml. S. Bryant, Minister.
Oct. 28, 1848	Watkins, Thomas, and Lucindy Patterson. Geo. W. McNeely, Minister.
Oct. 12, 1826	Watson, Davis, and Nancy Caton. William Davis, Minister.
Return dated Nov. 9, 1847	Watson, Davis, and Eliza Gibson. Joseph H. Eanes, Minister.
Aug. 7, 1785	Watson, Elexander, and Elizabeth Willis. Robert Jones, Minister.
Dec. 5, 1848	Watt, William P., and Sallie S. Dillard, at house of Col. Peter H. Dillard. W. N. Mebane, Minister.
Return dated Dec. 24, 1819	Weakly, Joseph, and Elizabeth Leak. Maning Hill, Minister.
May 16, 1831	Weaver, Benjamin, and Nancy Leake. Maning Hill, Minister.
Oct. 9, 1833	Weaver, James C., and Martha Nunn. A. Walker, Minister.
Sept. 10, 1825	Weaver, Joseph C., and Sarah Leake. Othniel Minter, Minister.
May 11, 1813	Webb, Robert, and Elizabeth Thacker. Lewis Foster, Minister.
Nov. - 1825	Wells, Edmund P., and Mary M. Hughes. Arnold Walker, Minister.
Undated	Wells, Edward, and America Griffen. Silas Minter, Minister.
Sept. 18, 1828	Wells, Francis, and Sarah Smith. Arnold Walker, Minister.

May 4, 1809	Wells, George P., and Nancy Petty. William Blair, Minister.
Dec. 15, 1846	Wells, John, and Matilda Wells. Wm. M. Schoolfield, Minister.
Return dated Nov. 9, 1818	Wells, Sterling, and Patsy Dillen. John C. Traylor, Minister.
Dec. 19, 1824	Wells, Thomas, and Milly Chishenhall. Othniel Minter, Minister.
Dec. 23, 1847	Wells, Thomas, and Susan Cole, dau. of Hamblen Cole. James M. Wilson, Minister.
Nov. 21, 1848	Wells, Thomas P., and Elizabeth Wells. Wm. M. Schoolfield, Minister.
July 24, 1828	Wells, William C., and Lucy A. Hughes. Maning Hill Minister.
Oct. 12, 1844	Wells, William Burwell, and Nancy Morris. William Schoolfield, Minister.
Dec. 26, 1792	Wheat, Benjamin, and Patsey Chavis (?). Joseph Anthony, Minister.
Sept. 26, 1787	Whittington, William, and Rhoda Maning. Joseph Anthony, Minister.
Nov. - 1823	Wiatt, Craven, and Eleanor Richardson. Arnold Walker, Minister.
Mar. 21, 1787	Wilkerson, David, and Elizabeth King. Joseph Anthony, Minister.
Nov. 16, 1809	Williams, Joseph, and Sally Proctor. James Patterson, Minister.
July 28, 1842	Williams, Joseph N., and Nancy Mills. Othniel Minter, Minister.
Oct. - 1841	Williams, Robert W., and Elizabeth P. Martin. A. Walker, Minister.
Return dated July 24, 1783	Williams, Silas, and Lucy Haley. William Lovell, Minister.
July 21, 1836	Williams, Thomas, and Elizabeth Mills. Othniel Minter, Minister.
Jan. 5, 1781	Willis, David, and Mary Cook. Peter Smith, Minister.
Return dated June 25, 1844	Willis, Robert W., and Mary Jarrott. Joseph H. Evans, Minister.
Dec. 23, 1845	Wilmouth, William, and Susan Thomas.

Feb. 26, 1829	Wilson, Aaron, and Sarah Gilly. William Davis, Minister.
Oct. 27, 1833	Wilson, Aaron, and Ann Dyer. A. Walker, Minister.
Return dated July 12, 1842	Wilson, Andrew, and Betsey S. Moore.
Nov. 8, 1835	Wilson, Bartlett, and Susan Haily. William Davis, Minister.
Mar. 30, 1843	Wilson, Burwell, and Perrizida Mahon. Arthur W. Eanes, Minister.
Return dated Nov. 9, 1847	Wilson, Jackson, and Rhoda V. Watson. Joseph H. Eanes, Minister.
Dec. 6, 1789	Wilson, James, and Martha Hix. Joseph Anthony, Minister.
Return dated Nov. 9, 1847	Wilson, James, and Caroline Gilly. Joseph H. Eanes, Minister.
July 31, 1834	Wilson, Jeams, and Nancy Turner.
Return dated Mar. 18, 1815	Wilson, John, and Lucy Fortune (?). William Davis, Minister.
July 29, 1840	Wilson, Morgan, and Martha Odle.
Nov. 26, 1836	Wilson, William, and Charity Jones. Othniel Minter, Minister.
Feb. 8, 1844	Wilson, William, and Sarah McDaniel. Othneil Minter, Minister.
Dec. 22, 1825	Winn, Joseph, and Elizabeth Anderson. Maning Hill, Minister.
Return dated May 13, 1816	Witt, Daniel, and Martha Brewer. John C. Taylor, Minister.
Dec. 19, 1789	Witt, Joel, and Mary Taylor. Joseph Anthony, Minister.
Return dated July 24, 1783	Witt, John, and Dicey Holland. William Lovell, Minister.
--- - 1783	Witt, William, and Elizabeth Haley. William Lovell, Minister.
Jan. 12, 1821	Wood, Moses, and Elizabeth M. Smith. John C. Traylor, Minister.
Apr. 9, 1827	Woodall, Christopher T., and Margarett Simes. Othniel Minter, Minister.
Apr. 14, 1782	Woods, John, and Lucy Hawkins. Peter Smith, Minister.

Return dated
July 27, 1806   Woodson, Benjamin, and Patsey Lasure. John King, Minister.

Nov. - 1835   Woody, Allen, and Ann Williamson. Arnold Walker, Minister.

Oct. 27, 1785   Woody, Martin, and Susanna Roberson. Robert Jones, Minister.

Dec. 16, 1783   Woody, Wm., and Jean Small. John Newman, Minister.

Return dated
1830   Wooton, John T., and Lucy Redd. John C. Traylor, Minister.

Dec. 18, 1823   Wright, Daniel O., and Elizabeth Pulliam. Orson Martin, Minister.

Nov. 16, 1834   Wright, James, and Lucy Goodman. Othniel Minter, Minister.

Return dated
Feb. 11, 1839   Wyatt, Craven, and Nancy Eggleton. Silas Minter, Minister.

Sept. 6, 1829   Wyatt, Saunders, and Rachel Delozier. Othneil Minter, Minister.

Dec. - 1846   Wyatt, Wesley S., and Lucinda Thomas. John R. Martin, Minister.

Nov. 18, 1810   Young, David, and Nelly Humphrey. Maning Hill, Minister.

Undated   ------, Simeon C., and Amelia Tyson. Silas Minter, Minister.

June 18, 1792   -----, -----, and Louise Pace (?). Joseph Anthony, Minister.

* 9 7 8 0 8 0 6 3 0 7 0 2 2 *

HENRY COUNTY, VIRGINIA, MARRIAGE BONDS, 1778-1849

Compiled by
VIRGINIA ANDERTON DODD

CLEARFIELD

Originally Published
Richmond, Virginia
1953

Reprinted with Permission of the Compiler
Genealogical Publishing Co., Inc.
Baltimore, 1976

Reprinted for
Clearfield Company, Inc. by
Genealogical Publishing Co., Inc.
Baltimore, Maryland
1989, 1996

Library of Congress Catalogue Card Number 75-34714
International Standard Book Number 0-8063-0702-1

Reprinted from a volume in
The North Carolina State Library
Raleigh, North Carolina

Made in the United States of America